Pāṇini to Patañjali

Pāṇini to Patañjali

— A Grammatical March —

Edited by
Bidyut Lata Ray

DK PRINTWORLD
Publishers of Indian Traditions

Cataloging in Publication Data — DK

Pāṇini to Patañjali : a grammatical march / edited by Bidyut Lata Ray. – Second impression.
pages cm
Contributed articles.
"First Published in India in 2004" – Title page verso.
Includes bibliographical references and index.
ISBN 9788124602478

1. Sanskrit language – Grammar. 2. Pāṇini. Aṣṭādhyāyī. 3. Patañjali. Mahābhāṣya. I. Rāya, Bidyutlatā, editor.

LCC PK519.P36 2021 | DDC 491.25 23

ISBN 978-81-246-0247-8
First Published in India in 2004
Second impression published in 2021

Published and printed by:
D.K. Printworld (P) Ltd.
Regd. office : Vedaśrī, F-395, Sudarshan Park
(Metro Station: ESI Hospital), New Delhi - 110015
Phones : (011) 2545 3975, 2546 6019
E-mail: indology@dkprintworld.com
Website: www.dkprintworld.com

Forewording Note

I am glad to know that you are bringing out a scholarly research work entitled: "Pāṇini to Patañjali: A Grammatical March." The list of the chapters of your forthcoming publication clearly shows that this learned work will definitely prove useful to all students of Sanskrit interested in the Pāṇinian Grammar. I send my best wishes to all the learned contributors of this scholarly work.

31.7.03

Dr. Ram Gopal
(Former Vice-Chancellor
M.D. University, Rohtak)
3051, Sector 21-D,
Chandigarh-160 022

Preface

THE present treatise *'Pāṇini to Patañjali : A Grammatical March'* is composed of eight scholarly contributions, spreading over the origin and development of Sanskrit grammar during the period in question. This volume is unique in nature as it deals with thought-provoking areas of grammatical sense, starting from its very inception to the work of Patañjali. The *Aṣṭādhyāyī* of Pāṇini, the *Vārttika*s of Kātyāyana and the *Mahābhāṣya* of Patañjali, being monumental works of Sanskrit grammar, are the main attractions of our depressions here. The literature is, no doubt, replete with copious commentaries and interpretations on Sanskrit grammar, still a benevolent attempt has been made in this book to present a concise analysis of the systems of Sanskrit grammar from Pāṇini to Patañjali.

The projected study begins with the general introduction covering a considerable amount of the information about the origin and development of Sanskrit grammar from the period of the Vedas to the period of the *Mahābhāṣya*. Evidently, Chapter 1 deals with the preliminaries to the discussions, undertaken in the subsequent chapters. It throws light on the path of the grammatical march led by Pāṇini, Kātyāyana and Patañjali.

The study included in Chapter 1 has been further enlarged by Sri Krutibas Rath in Chapter 2 where the genesis of Sanskrit grammar has been critically analysed with the true sense of its technical terms. Sri Rath has tried to his best to design a relatively full picture of the extensive and insightful thinking about the grammatical literature under discussion.

The topic of Pāṇini's contribution to Sanskrit grammar has been taken up for discussion by Dr. Shankar Nene in Chapter 3. Here, the author has comprehensively treated the Pāṇinian system of Sanskrit grammar, focusing on its style and technicalities.

In Chapter 4, Dr. P. Narayan Namboodiri explains the technical devices present in the *Aṣṭādhyāyī* of Pāṇini. According to the author, there are about four thousand *sūtras*, found in the *Aṣṭādhyāyī*, examining the correctness of the words and their derivation, in detail.

Development of Sanskrit grammar after Pāṇini has been discussed by Dr. Yoshiyuki Iwasaki in Chapter 5. Here, the author presents, chronologically, the systems of Sanskrit grammar pertaining to various schools, emerged after Pāṇini. Among such schools, those of Kātyāyana and Patañjali, are noteworthy. Besides the style and system of the *Vārttikas*, the author hints at the philosophical doctrine of Kātyāyana, i.e., "eternity of the words." The *Mahābhāṣya* of Patañjali adheres to the conversational style of expressions with typical arguments. Iwasaki holds that Patañjali merely enumerates various opinions, without giving a decisive conclusion, and merely expresses the necessity of further investigation. A discussion on the philosophy of language forms another component of Iwasaki's investigation on Sanskrit grammar, after Pāṇini.

In Chapter 6, Dr. Malhar Kulkarni makes an attempt to study the contributions of Kātyāyana to the Pāṇinian grammar. He has also tried to take a survey of the works, done by the modern scholars, since the last two centuries, in this regard. The author has made two basic approaches, traditional and Western, (to focus) on the topic. Both these approaches have peculiarities of their own, which present them in different perspectives. The prime contribution of Kātyāyana to the grammar of Pāṇini is the incorporation of the element of the philosophy of language. According to the author, Kātyāyana was the first to interpret the difficult words in the *Aṣṭādhyāyī* on the basis of the philosophical doctrine.

Chapter 7 presents the grammar of Patañjali, the *bhāṣyakāra*. Here, Prof. Saroja Bhate enumerates the tradition and technique of Patañjali's *Vyākaraṇa Mahābhāṣya*. According to her, the *Mahābhāṣya* is the foundation of post-Pāṇinian systems of Sanskrit grammar. It appears as the keystone of the whole grammatical structure, based on Pāṇini. Prof. Bhate makes attempts to highlight some of the salient features of Patañjali's works, like its style, language, logic, linguistic debates and discourses, the *sūtra*s and their scientific interpretation, the semantics and the realm of metaphysics *et seq*.

In Chapter 8, Dr. Jatindramohan Mishra reviews the date of Patañjali, following the discussions by different scholars over a couple of centuries, on the topic. The author's discourse, here, deals with the opinions of some prominent scholars, like T. Goldstücker, R.G. Bhandarkar, S.D. Joshi, B.N. Puri and Yudhiṣṭhira Mīmāṁsaka on the date of Patañjali. Adhering to Prof. Joshi's dating of the *Mahābhāṣya*, Dr. Mishra leans to accept that the upper limit of Patañjali is 85 BC.

Thus, the post-Pāṇinian systems of Sanskrit grammar have been well-exercised in the works of Kātyāyana and Patañjali, which actually have shown the path for understanding the Pāṇinian rules in the true sense of its grammatical and linguistic terms. The other works, included in the post-Pāṇinian systems of Sanskrit grammar, are those of Kātantra, Cāndra, Jainendra, Śākaṭāyana, Sarasvatīkaṇṭhābharaṇa, Sārasvata, Mugdhabodha, Haima, Saṁkṣiptasāra and Supadma Vayākaraṇa, et seq. As the present work restricts itself only to the development of Sanskrit grammar from Pāṇini to Patañjali, the other works after Pāṇini have not been included, here. However, these contributions have been comprehensively treated by Dr. R.S. Saini in his book, *Post-Pāṇinian Systems of Sanskrit Grammar*.

Here, in this treatise, our authors have tried their level best to gather their ideas and reflections on the grammatical march, led by the *trimuni* — Pāṇini, Kātyāyana and Patañjali in every aspect of *Śabdānuśāsana*. Such a long cherished project would not have seen the dawn of the day without the imprints and attentions of our learned grammarians.

Dr. (Mrs) Bidyut Lata Ray

Contents

Acknowledgements

THE real architects of this project are our contributors. I owe my indebtedness to all of them. Specifically, I am highly obliged to Prof. Saroja Bhate for the sustained interest in the present work. This small treatise bears the stamp of her ungrudging help and co-operation for its successful completion.

I am highly indebted to my loving parents, in-laws and revered teachers, who fostered fortification of the fulcrum of my research fascinations.

I am very much thankful to my friends and well-wishers for their constant inspirations and encouragements.

It is inadequate to express my sincere gratefulness to my husband and children who have cheerfully and gracefully helped me during the period of my work. My husband, Dr. Sadasiva Biswal, Reader in Physics, Nayagarh College, Nayagarh, helped me, both, concretely, with his editorial acumen and, more generally, by providing me the facilities without which my efforts would have remained fruitless. From beginning to end, he has been my ground and the support.

I am highly indebted to the authors and publishers, from whose works I have drawn enough material for this compilation.

Last but not the least, I am ever grateful to Mr. Susheel K. Mittal, Director, D.K. Printworld (P) Ltd., New Delhi, for bringing out this monograph in a magnificent style of printing and attractive get-up.

Dr. (Mrs.) Bidyut Lata Ray

Abbreviations

ALS	:	Adyar Library Series, Chennai
AV	:	*Atharvaveda*
BORI	:	Bhandarkar Oriental Research Institute
CASS	:	Centre of Advanced Studies in Sanskrit, Pune
Cf.	:	Confer (= compare)
fn.	:	Footnote
Gov. OS	:	Government Oriental Series (The abbreviation is followed by a class letter)
IA	:	*Indian Antiquary*
Ibid.	:	*Ibidem*
IHQ	:	*Indian Historical Quarterly*
JAOS	:	*Journal of the American Oriental Society*, New Haven
JAS	:	*Journal of Asiatic Society*, Bombay
JOIB	:	*Journal of Oriental Institute*, Baroda
JOR	:	*Journal of Oriental Research*, Madras
MLBD	:	Motilal Banarsidass, Delhi
Op.cit	:	*Opere Citato* (= in the work quoted)

ṚV	:	*Ṛgveda*
SJSU	:	Śrī Jagannātha Sanskrit University, Purī.
VIJ	:	*Vishveshvarananda Indological Journal*, Hoshiarpur, Punjab
ZII	:	*Zeitschrift für Indologie und Iranistik*, Leipzig

1

Prolegomenon

Bidyut Lata Ray

THE origin of Sanskrit grammar owes to the Vedas. In fact, the comprehensive system of the Vedas is called grammar (*vyākaraṇa*). Yāska[1] has pointed out that the development of the various stages of knowledge has emanated from the Vedas. In order to understand the Vedic words and terms clearly, the Vedāṅgas are created. According to the ancient seers, the Vedāṅgas were written with a view to acquainting people with the meanings of the Vedas.

The major Vedāṅgas are of six types: Vyākaraṇa (grammar), Chandas (prosody), Nirukta (etymology), Śikṣa (phonetics) Jyotiṣa (astronomy) and Kalpa.

The fist mention of the auxiliary systems called, Vedāṅgas, is found in the *Ṣaḍviṁśa Brāhmaṇa*.[2] Max Müller admits this while considering the verse *prakṣipta*.[3] These six branches of knowledge are helpful in understanding the Vedārtha.[4] Śikṣā and Chandas help in the correct pronunciation of the Vedas. Vyākaraṇa and the Nirukta are useful for the full comprehension of the Vedic verses. For the performance of

1. *Nirukta,* 1.20.
2. *Ṣaḍvimśa Brāhmaṇa,* 4.7.
3. *History of Sanskrit Literature,* p. 57.
4. Sāyaṇa, *Ṛgbhāṣya,* p. 57.

sacrifices and rituals, the ancient seers were taking the help of Kalpa and Jyotiṣa.[5] Out of these six Vedāṅgas, Vyākaraṇa has been accorded pride of place by scholars. Since we fully depend on grammar to know the meanings of the words, the scholars have rightly considered this branch of knowledge as the supreme element.[6] The difference between the classical and the Vedic language led scholars to think of the relationship between the word and its meaning and this resulted in the birth of grammar.[7]

The antiquity of grammar is very old. In the true sense, Vyākaraṇa means *Śabdaśāstra* which is gleaned from our ancient texts like the *Vālmīkīya Rāmāyaṇa, Gopatha Brāhmaṇa, Muṇḍakopaniṣad*, the *Mahābhārata, et seq.*[8] Actually, grammar springs up from Brahmā to the succeeding generations of grammarians: Brahmā to Bṛhaspati, Bṛhaspati to Indra, Indra to Bhāradvāja, Bhāradvāja to *ṛṣis*, and to brāhmaṇas. This goes in support of the opinion of Patañjali[9] that Bṛhaspati transferred each word to Indra for over thousand years. According to the *Taittirīya Saṁhitā*[10] and its commentator, Sāyaṇa,[11] Indra is considered as the first purifier of grammar. Pt. Yudhiṣṭhira Mīmāṁsaka,[12] an eminent Sanskrit scholar, accepts this view.

Śikṣā and Prātiśākhyas

The work *śikṣā* means lesson, because *śikṣā* teaches the method

---

5. *A History of Indian Literature*, p. 268.
6. Haradatta, *Padamañjarī*, Part I, p. 7.
7. Avanindra Kumar, *Archaic Words in Pāṇini*'s *Aṣṭādhyāyī*, Parimal Publications, Delhi, 1981, p. 3.
8. *Ibid.*, p. 4 and fn. 6.
9. *Mahābhāṣya*, Paspaśahnika.
10. *Taittirīya Saṁhitā*, 6.4.7.
11. Sāyaṇa, *Ṛgbhāṣyopodghāta*, Poona, I, p. 26.
12. *Sanskrit Vyākaraṇa Śāstra Kā Itihāsa*, edn. Part I, pp. 58-62.

of pronunciation, of the vocal organs and the physical effort involved in the producation of phonemes. Briefly, it can be stated that Śikṣā texts teach everything connected with the oratorial study of the Vedas. Śikṣās are almost inextricably connected with Prātiśākhyas, which are modifications of Śikṣās in the various schools. Technically, Śikṣās are Vedāṅga; Prātiśākhayas are not but it is not possible to treat the one without the help of the other.

The *Taittirīya Upaniṣad* defines Śikṣā as concerned with syllables, accents, length of vocables, stresses, chants and euphonic combinations; all Śikṣās take up these subjects.[13] Besides, major Śikṣās, like the Pāṇinīya, go deeper into subjects like the sources of vocables, and oral accoustics of pronunciations. The Prātiśākhyas, on the other hand, approach the subject from its audial aspect. Prātiśākhyas deal mainly with *uccārana* (tone) *svara, sandhi* and the *padapāṭha*. Since these texts contain the subject-matter of Śikṣā *granthas* and Vyākaraṇa *granthas*, at certain places, scholars mention them only by the word *śikṣā*.[14] Winternitz opines that the Prātisākhyas are the earliest representatives of the Vedāṅga *śikṣā*.[15] According to M.M. Ghosha,[16] the development of Śikṣā Vedāṅga took place first and, then, Prātiśākhyas were developed. The Prātiśākhyas, belonging as they do to the second age of the study of the Śikṣā Vedāṅga, had a much wider scope than the manual of the subject, that was produced in the first age. From a study of the contents of the Prātiśākhyas, we find that the scope of the Śikṣā, as given in

13. S. Bhattacharji, *Literature in the Vedic Age*, Vol. 2, K.P. Bagchi & Company, Calcutta, 1986, p. 291.

14. Viṣṇumitra, *Ṛk Prātiśakhya*, quoted in "Archaic words in Pāṇini's Aṣṭādhyāyī," by Dr. Avanindra Kumar, p. 5 and fn. 4.

15. M. Winternitz, *A History of Indian Literature*, Vol. I, p. 285.

16. M.M. Ghosha, *Pāṇinīya Śikṣā*, Introd., p. xxxviii.

the *Taittirīyopanisad*[17], applies to a considerable extent to the Prātiśākhyas, which should be called secondary Śikṣā.[18] The tables of contents are almost the same for its Śikṣās and Prātisākhyas — although the former is concerned more with the nature of the articulation effort and the latter with the product, i.e., the sound of the finished phonemes.

Pāṇinīya Śikṣā was, most probably, the only Śikṣā that existed, initially. This Śikṣā, being the oldest text of Vedic phonetics, underwent modification, over a long time, and, from place to place, Ostensibly, the *Taittirīya Āraṇyaka*[19] uses Śikṣā in the singular. This may also have been a genre name which covers a number of individual texts of different schools. The Śikṣā texts which have come down to us must be placed near the earliest periods of Vedāṅga *sūtras*, while the Prātiśākhyas were later by four to three centuries; the latest Prātiśākhyas probably belong to the second century BC.[20]

Prātiśakhyas and Vyākaraṇa

The nature and the subject-matter of the Prātiśākhyas reveal that these works contain much that would normally be called grammar in spite of their overlapping of their subjects to a great extent. But, V.V. Sarma[21] opines that the Prātiśākhyas are never called Vyākaraṇa because their real object is not to teach the grammar of language, but to enumerate the perfect system of different Vedic schools. Yet, they clearly presuppose the existence and cultivation of grammar and anticipate the separation of the two into distinct disciplines. Bhattacharji

17. *Taittirīyopaniṣad*, 1.2.
18. M.M. Ghosha, *op.cit.*, p. xxxviii.
19. *Taittirīya Āraṇyaka*, VIII, 2.1.
20. S. Bhattacharji, *op. cit.*, p. 294.
21. V.V. Sarma, *Critical Studies on Kātyāyana*'s *Śuklayajurveda-prātiśākhya*, Madras, 1935, p. 80.

holds that the language used in the Prātiśākhyas is more fluid, with innumerable local variations in pronunciation, intonation, euphonic combinations and accent. With the emergence of grammar as a distinct subject, these are more rigidly codified.[22]

The etymology of the word *vyākaraṇa* has been derived from *vyākṛti,* which means division into *prakṛti* and *pratyaya.*[23] Following this derivation, T. Goldstücker says —

> *Vyākaraṇa* means undoing, i.e., analysis and Pāṇini's grammar is intended to be a linguistic analysis; it undoes words and undoes sentences, which consist of words; it examines the component parts of a word.[24]

Vyākaraṇa is also the synonymous of *Śabdānuśāsana.* Hardatta's view goes in favour of this.[25] The meaning of a word can be easily followed from its *prakṛti* and *pratyaya.* This view has been accepted by Nāgeśa in *Laghumañjūṣā.*[26] According to Bhartṛhari, Vyākaraṇa is a Smṛti, which establishes the correctness of words whether classical, colloquial or Vedic.[27] Further, Bhartṛhari has given eight meanings of the word *smṛti.*[28] Ācārya Durgā has indicated eight kinds of grammar.[29]

There are differences between the Prātiśakhya and the

---

22. S. Bhattacharji, *op. cit.,* p. 297.
23. Avanindra Kumar, *op. cit.,* p. 6 and fn. 3.

    Patañjali has given the etymology of the words *vyākaraṇa* as — "व्याक्रियन्ते शब्दा अनेनेति" — *MB. Paspaśāhnika.*
24. T. Goldstücker, *Pāṇini, His Place in Sanskrit Literature,* London, Trübner, 1861, and Reprint, Allahabad, The Pāṇini Office, 1914.
25. Comp. *Śabdakaustubha,* pp. 6 and *Uddyota,* p. 5
26. *Laghumañjūṣā,* pp. 5, 6.
27. Bhartṛhari, *Vākyapadīya,* 1.24.
28. *Ibid.*
29. *Nirukta,* 1.20: व्याकरणमष्टधा.

Vyākaraṇa. Dr. Varma is of the opinion that the original and, perhaps, the more significant term for the Prātiśākhya was the *pārṣada* and the commentators, sometimes, speak of the *Ṛg* Prātiśākhya as *pārṣada*.[30] Again, three words, *caraṇa*, *śākhā* and *pārṣada*, exist to denote different ways of learning. The word, *caraṇa*, has been used in the Nirukta,[31] in the *Aṣṭādhyāyī*, in the *Mahābhāṣya*[33] and other works. Ācārya Durgā[34] thinks that *caraṇa* means *śākhā*. According to Max Müller,[35] however, *śākhā* means, originally, a literary work which *caraṇa* does not indicate. Jinedrabuddhi[36] opines that *śākhā* means a branch of learning as well as the persons who go through it. Kaiyaṭa and Haradatta[37] say that the word *caraṇa* has been used to denote the learners of that branch. It is also clear from the *Nyāsa* that there exists various types of *caraṇa* to differentiate between different ways of learning.[38] Ostensibly, by the word *caraṇa* the ancient scholars meant a particular branch of learning and its readers. A group of learners of different *śākhā*s and same *caraṇa*s of a particular *śāstra* is known as *pārṣad*.[39]

Prātiśākhyas deals with the principles related to *varṇoccāraṇa*, *padapāṭha*, *kramapāṭha*, *sandhi* and *svara*. Besides these, the *Taittirīya* Prātiśākhya also deals with *Jaṭāpāṭha* and the *Ṛk* Prātiśākhya with the examination of meters. On the basis of the subject matter of the Prātiśākhyas, they are included by

30. S. Varma, *The Phonetic*, p. 12.
31. *Nirukta*, 1.17.
32. *Aṣṭādhyāyī*, II. 4.3; IV. 2.46; IV. 3.126; V. 1.134; VI. 3.86.
33. *Mahābhāṣya*, IV. 3.12.
34. *Nirukta*, 1.17.
35. Max Müller, *History of Sanskrit Literature*, p. 65
36. *Nyāsa*, II. 4.3.
37. *Pradīpa*, *Pada* IV. 1.63.
38. *Ibid*.
39. Avanindra Kumar, *op. cit.*, p. 10.

some scholars in the Śikṣā Vedāṅga; and, by some others, in Vyākaraṇa Vedāṅga. The inclusion of the Prātiśākhyas in both the Vedāṅgas has been supported by Uvvaṭācārya.[40]

Gārgya Gopāl Yajvas' view also goes in favour of this.[41] According to Dr. Avanindra Kumar,[42] Prātiśākhya is like grammar, nevertheless, there is some difference. The Prātiśākhya deals with certain special principles (*vidhis*) in some particular *caraṇa* and does not prove the correctness of the word by grammatical analysis as is done in the Vyākaraṇa. The authors of the Prātiśākhyas were well-acquainted with grammar. Banfey remarked that these authors attained the high stature in the field of grammar. According to him, "the Prātiśākhyas are based on grammar of a very advanced stage."[43]

Schools of Grammar

There exists at least, twelve schools of grammar, with over three hundred grammarians and more than a thousand works.[44] According to S.K. Belvalker,[45]

> on the lowest calculation, there are, yet, current, in various parts of India, nearly a dozen different schools of Sanskrit Grammar, at least, three hundred writers in the field, including those that are known to us only from quotations and more than thousand separate treatises original as well as explanatory.

40. *Vājasaneyī Prātiśakhya*, 1.69, Uvvaṭācārya's Bhāṣya.
41. *Taittirīya Prātiśakhya*, 1.21, *Vaidikābharaṇa Bhāṣya.*
42. Avanindra Kumar, *op.cit.*, p. 12.
43. S. Varma, *The Contributions to Phonetics by Ancient Grammarians*, p. 15.
44. Avanindra Kumar, *op.cit.*, p. 14.
45. S.K. Belvalker, *Systems of Sanskrit Grammar*, Poona, 1915, p. 1.

The most complete history of Sanskrit grammarians, written to date, is that of Yudhiṣṭhira Mīmāṁsakā,[46] in which are treated all important questions of chronologies and text attributions, with very full documentations.[47] *Kavikalpadruma*[48] of Bopadeva mentions the names of eight grammarians. There is mention of nine works on the Vyākaraṇa in the *Śrītattvanidhi*.[49] The twelve schools of grammar, prevailing during time of Belvalker are Pāṇinīya, Cāndra, Jainedra, Śākaṭāyana, Haimacandra, Kātantra, Sārasvata, Bopadevīya, Jaumār, Saupadma, Harināmāmṛta and Prabodhaprakāśa.[50] The qualities of Pāṇinīya grammar supersede all other schools of grammar. Madhusudan Sarasvati[51] considers Pāṇini's grammar as a Vedāṅga.

In the *Aṣṭāḍhyāyī*, Pāṇini mentions, by name, ten other persons, all presumably grammarians. They are Āpiśali, Kāśyapa, Gārgya, Gālava, Cakravarman, Bhāradvāja, Śākaṭāyana, Śākalya, Senaka and Sphoṭāyana. The most complete survey of information on these appears in Yudhiṣṭhira Mīmāṁsaka.[53] Most modern scholars have recognized that Pāṇini's mention of other grammarians serves to convey differences in usage; and when the name of another

46. *Daśapādyuṇādivṛtti*, Government Sanskrit College, Banaras, 1943, p. 1.
47. G. Cardona, *Pāṇini: A Survey of Research*, Motilal Banarsidass, Delhi, 1980, p. 139.
48. *Sanskṛta Vyākaraṇa Śāstra kā Itihāsa*, Sonepat, 1973, Part I, p. 14.
49. *Ibid.*, p. 65.
50. Avanindra Kumar, *op. cit.*, p. 14.
51. *Prasthānabheda*, p. 78.
52. Possibly in a broad sense, including observers of differences in usage of course, even observations of such differences imply grammatical awareness.
53. Yudhiṣṭhira Mīmāṁsaka, 1973, Part I, pp. 134-77.

grammarian is coupled with a term such as *vā*, the rule in question states an optional operation, recognized by that grammarian.[54] Pāṇini has used the terms *udīcām* and *prācām* meaning, thereby, northerners and easterners, respectively. The commentators consider that both terms refer to areas in which certain usages obtain and to school of grammarians. Ostensibly, Pāṇini refers to schools of grammar. Many modern scholars have also accepted this.[55] It is thus clear that other grammarians, predecessors or contemporaries of Pāṇini, had, like him, noted particular usages Pāṇini used in his own work. Moreover, it is also evident from the *Mahābhāṣya* of Patañjali that, at the time of Kātyāyana and Patañjali, grammars by Āpiśali and Śākaṭāyana were known. Kātyāyana cites the utterance, *āpiśalam adhīte,* and "studies the grammar of Āpiśali."[56] Patañjali has also noted that the above phrase conveys the meaning of the derivate *āpiśalā* (brāḥmaṇī), a brāhmaṇa woman who studies Āpiśali's grammar.[57] Besides, Patañjali refers to a rule (*vidhi*) of Āpiśali[58], according to which the term *dhenu* (cow) is followed by the affix *ka* to form the derivative *dhainuka* (group of cows), unless it is preceded by the negative particle. Moreover, Patañjali refers to grammars, promulgated (*prokta*) by Pāṇini, Āpiśali and Kāśakṛtsna — *pāṇininā proktam pāṇinīyam, āpiśalam, kāśakṛtsnam.*[59] And a verse cited in the *Mahābhāṣya* on 3.3.1 refers to Śakaṭāyana as the grammarian who held that all nouns were derived from

54. G. Cardona, *op.cit.*, p. 146.

55. *Ibid.*, p. 147.

56. Vārttika 3 on 4.1.14.

L.F. Kielhorn, *The Vyākaraṇa-mahābhāṣya of Patañjali*, 3 Vols., Government Central Press, Bombay, 1880-85, II.205.20.

57. *Ibid.*, 205. 3.

58. Yudhiṣṭhira Mīmāṁsaka, *op.cit.*, 1973, I.139-40.

59. L.F. Kielhorn, *op.cit.*, I.12.5.6.

verbs.[60] The term *pūrva-sūtra* used by Kātyāyana and Patañjali refers to earlier (*pūrva*) grammars.[61]

Moreover, Pāṇini, himself, occasionally, uses terms which he has not introduced in his own rules. For example, he, himself, introduces the accurative dual-ending *au* with the appended maker *ṭ* (*auṭ*). But, in the rule 7.1.18 (*auria āpaḥ*), he uses the term *auri* to refer to the nominative and accusative dual-endings *au*, thus, making use of a marker *ri* attached to *au*. Patañjali considers this as a term from a *pūrva-sūtra*.[62]

Thus, it is revealed that Pāṇini, indeed, had predecessors in the field of grammar.

Schools of Prātiśākhyas

The Prātiśākhyas, available these days, refer to 95 different *ācāryas*. The dates of the Prātiśākhyas were later than the Śikṣā texts by four to three, centuries. The latest Prātiśākhyas, probably, belong to the second century BC. The available Prātiśākhyas can be categorized under the broadlines of *Ṛk*, *Vājasaneyī*, *Taittirīya*, *Maitrāyaṇīya*, *Sāma* and *Atharva*. Besides these, some other Prātiśākhyas are known with different characters. Such works are eight in number. According to Pt. Mīmāṁsaka,[63] four Prātiśākhyas have been in the name of Āśvalāyana, Vāṣkala, Śānkhāyana and Cārāyaṇīya.

Presently available Prātiśākhya texts are Śaunak's *R̥k Prātiśākhya*, the *Taittirīya Prātiśākhya* of the *Yajurveda*, Kātyāyana's *Vājasaneya Prātiśākhya* of the *Śukla Yajurveda*,

---

60. *Ibid.*, II.138.16 Also, I.164.67.

61. L.F. Kielhorn, *Notes on the Mahābhāṣya*, IA 16, 101.06. Yudhiṣṭhira Mīmāṁsaka, *op.cit.*, 1973, I.241.

62. L.F. Kielhorn, ed., *The Vyākaraṇa-mahābhāṣya of Patañjali*, 3 Vols., Government Press, Bombay, 1880-85, III.247.12.

63. *Sanskrit Vyākaraṇa Śāstra Kā Itihāsa*, Part I, pp. 69-72.

Śaunaka's *Atharva Prātiśākhya* (or *Caturādhyāyikā*) of the Atharvaveda and the *Sāma Prātiśākhya* (to which are appended short texts like the *puṣpa* or *pañcavidhasūtra*).[64] There exist a number of Prātiśākhyas belonging to various regions as well as to different schools. Some of them are older than the others. From Uvvaṭa's commentary, it is known that Prātiśākhya is a collation of aphorisms common to the Śikṣās, *chanda*s and Vyākaraṇas of all the Vedas and a modification of these general rules according to usages of particular schools (*śākhā*s) and hence, the word *prātiśākhya*. Evidently, the *Ṛk Prātiśākhya* signifies itself as a Vedāṅga (xix.69) although the familiar list includes *śikhā,* presumably, because that list was compiled after *śikhā*s which were formed out of Prātiśākhyas. Śikṣās have been included in Prātiśākhyas by Uvvaṭa, who has named the Prātiśākhyas as *pārṣada,* derived from *pariṣad,* the assembly of the learned.

Śaunaka's *Ṛk Prātiśākhya* bears 18 *paṭalas*, which belong to the Śākala school and are divided into two broad divisions. The first part consists of a section on the alphabet and the second contains lengthened vowels, varieties of the *plūta* accent, the *karma* mode of memorization, fixed position as of certain phonemes, rules for prefixes and indeclinables, compound phonemes, produced by euphonic combinations and suffixes, different speeds of recitations at different times, defective pronunciations, method of teaching pupils, meters, metric accents, exceptional types of *ṛk*s and complex meters and special rules regarding meters and eulogy of meters. According to S. Bhattacharji, the contents mentioned above are a fairly exhaustive treatment of grammar together with rudiments of phonetics — the earliest in the world.[65]

---

64. S. Bhattacharji, *Literature in the Vedic Age,* Vol. 2, K.P. Bagchi and Company, Calcutta 1986, p. 294.

65. *Ibid.,* p. 295.

In addition to the *Ṛk Prātiśākhya,* mentioned above, we have other Prātiśākhyas like *Taittirīya Prātiśākhya, Śukla Yajurveda Prātiśākhya* by Kātyāyana, *Sāmaveda Prātiśākhya* and the *Atharvaveda Prātiśākhya.* Out of the three Prātiśākhyas of the *Atharvaveda,* only one has come down to us as the *Atharva Prātiśākhya.*[66] The others, of the Śaunaka and Sāyaṇa schools have been left as the *Caturādhyāya,* while the third Prātiśākhya of the Paippalāda school is missing. From the testimony of Durgā, it is also evident that the Prātiśākhya related to more schools than one.[67] It has been suggested that the Prātiśākhyas relate to a group of *śākhās.*[68]

From the word *pārṣada,* we discover some clue to the solution of the problem whether Prātiśākhyas related to only one or all the *śākhās* of a Veda. For the Narāyaṇa's commentary to a passage (*ācāryaṁ sapariṣatkaṁ bhojayet sabrahmacāriṇaśca*) in the *Gobhila Gṛhyasūtra-bhāṣya,*[69] it has been made very much clear that students, belonging to different Vedic schools could take their lessons from one *ācārya.* The *ācārya,* together with his pupils, constituted a *pārṣada* or *pariṣad.* Evidently, Pārṣada-Sūtras related to such *pariṣadas,* comprising different schools of a Veda. Hence, it seems justifiable to arrive at the conclusion that Pārṣada-Sūtras or Prātiśākhyas related to each one or all the *śākhās* of a Veda.

Pāṇinīya-Śikṣā

The *Pāṇinīya-Śikṣā* is known as the Śikṣā-Vedāṅga. It contains

66. Surya Kant, *Atharvaprātiśākhyam,* Delhi, 1968, Introduction, p. 11.
67. M. Ghosh, *Pāṇinīya Śikṣā* (Text and Translation), V.K. Publishing House, Delhi, 1991, Introduction, p. xxxiii.
68. Max Müller, *History of Ancient Sanskrit Literature,* London, 1860, p. 131.
69. On the *Taittirīya Prātiśākhya,* IV.11; Siddheshwar Verma, *Critical Studies in the Phonetic Observation of Indian Grammarians,* London, 1929, p. 13.

only 18 couplets in *anuṣṭubh* meter though the longest recension includes no less than 42 additional couplets,[70] most of which are in the same meter. The *Pāṇinīya-Śikṣā* is, more or less, a complete manual on the pronunciation of the Vedic speech-sounds, in general.

The first two couplets of the *Pāṇinīya-Śikṣā* describes the speech-sounds (*varṇas*) with the mention of vowels and consonants, separately. The next four couplets adhere to the theory of production of the speech-sounds. This is followed by a five-fold classification of these sounds according to their pitch, quantity, place of articulation, primary effort (*prayatna*) and the secondary effort (*anupradāna*). In fact, the pitch and quantity are primarily concerned with the vowels while the other characteristics of sounds are associated with the remaining items of speech.

The language of *Pāṇinīya-Śikṣā* is nothing but the late form of Vedic speech. The presence of accent marks in the *Paṇinīya-Śikṣā* justifies the antiquity of the text. The *Pāṇiniya-Śikṣā* has been composed in the *anuṣṭubh* meter. Considering this, Max-Müller[71] speaks of the lateness of the text. On the basis of various factors, M. Ghosh[72] opines that the *anuṣṭubh* meter, in which the reconstructed *Pāṇinīya-Śikṣā* has been composed, appears, by no means, younger in age than that in which works, like *Bṛhaddevatā* (*c.* 400 BC), have been composed. The archaic nature of *Paṇinīya-Śikṣā* is gleaned from the characteristics of its 18 *śloka*s which have metrical, irregularity.

Pāṇinīya-Śikṣā reserves a place in the Indian literature. The

---

70. Some of the additional passages, e.g., *Ṛk* 46, 47 are not in verse. We, however, have called them couplets only as a matter of convenience Cf. M. Ghosh, *op.cit.*, p. xl.

71. Max Müller, *op.cit.*, p. 145.

72. M. Ghosh, *op.cit.*, p. xliii.

authors of this text or the *śikṣākāras*[73] are mentioned, once, in the commentary of Jaimini's *Pūrva-mīmāṁsā-sūtras* by Śabara (*c.* 500 AC).[74] Instead of quoting *Paṇinīya-Śikṣā*, here, Śabara has focused on its views. But, he discusses, later, on a theory of the production of words.[75] which is identical with that available in the *Paṇinīya-Śikṣā*.[76] Without mentioning any *śikṣā* or *śikṣākāra*, Bhartṛharī (*c.* 650 AC) too in his *Vākyapadīya* seems to follow the same theory.[77] Any concrete idea about the authorship of the *Paṇinīya-Śikṣā* is conceived from the works of Śabara and Bhatṛhari. Likewise, the works of Durgā (*c.* 1300 AC),[78] Sāyaṇa (1400 AC),[79] Someśvara[80] and Rāmakṛṣṇa[81] do not forward any definite idea about the date of composition of *Paṇinīya-Śikṣa*. On the other hand, Madhusūdana Sarasvati[82] (*c.* 1500 AC) as well as the author of the *Pārāśarī Śikṣā*[83] knew the *Paṇinīya-Śikṣā* as the Vedāṅga and knew Pāṇini as its author. The Śikṣā narrated in the *Śukranīti*[84] also reveals that the author of this work took the *Pāṇinīya-Śikṣā* as

73. Jaimini's *Pūrva-mīmāṁsā sūtras*, I.1.22.

74. R.G. Bhandarkar, *JBRAS*, 1914, p. 297 f.; M. Winternitz, *History of Indian Literature* Vol. III, p. 495.

75. Jaimini's *Pūrva-mīmāṁsā sūtras*, I.3.25.

76. *Pāṇinīya-śikṣa*, 3-6.

77. *Vākyapadīya*, I.47.

78. Durgā in his introduction to the comm. of the *Nirukta* quotes *Paṇinīya-śikṣā* from what he calls the *Vedāṅga Śikṣā* (see *Nirukta* in Bombay Skt. Series, p. 24) The date of the author is about 1300 AC (Introduction to the *Nirukta*, by Sarup, p. 50).

79. Max Müller, *op.cit.*, p. 122.

80. *Ibid.*

81. S. Verma, *Critical Studies in the Phonetic Observation of Indian Grammarians*, London, 1929, p. 5.

82. A. Weber, *Indische Studien*, p. 16.

83. *Śikṣā-saṁgraha*, p. 60.

84. M. Ghosh, *op.cit.*, p. xliv.

a Vedāṅga. Ostensibly, the eminent authorities, probably, from 500 AC to 1500 AC recognized the *Pāṇinīya-Śikṣa* as a Vedāṅga, concerned with all the Vedas. Still, some sounds like *ḷ* and *ḷh*, traced in some Vedic texts, do not occur at all in the *Pāṇinīya-Śikṣā* though they appear casually in the Prātiśākhyas. According to C.V. Vaidya, these sounds were non-existent in the Vedas and developed, later, due to Draviḍian influence.[85]

Relation Between Pāṇinīya-Śikṣā and Aṣṭādhyāyī

A comparison of the contents of the *Aṣṭādhyāyī* and the *Pāṇinīya-Śikṣā* reveals that Pāṇini is the author of the *Pāṇinīya-Śikṣā*. Such comparison goes as under:

(a) In the *Pāṇinīya-Śikṣā*, we find the uses of Pāṇinian *pratyāhāras*, such as *ac, car, ghaś, yaṇ, jaś, śar* and *hal*.

(b) *Ku, cu, ṭu, tu* and *pu* have been used to indicate, respectively, *k, c, ṭ, t* and *p* groups. This convention has been followed in the *Aṣṭādhyāyī*.[86]

(c) The *Pāṇinīya-Śikṣā* (17) includes the *anunāsika* into speech-sounds while its definition has been given in the *Aṣṭādhyāyī*.[87]

(d) The explanation of terms like *harsva, dīrgha* and *pluta* has also been given there in the *Aṣṭādhyāyī*.[88]

(e) According to a rule of *ṇa-tva*, as laid down in the *Aṣṭādhyāyī*,[89] *n* after *ṛ* and *ṣ* turns to *ṇ*. From this, we

---

85. C.V. Vaidya, *History of Sanskrit Literature*, Poona, 1930, Vol. I, Sec. I, p. 57; Sec. II, pp. 81, 114, 130, 137, 142, 154.

86. *Aṣṭādhyāyī*, I.1.69: *aṇudit savarṇasya cā pratyayaḥ*.

87. *Ibid.*, I.1.9: *mukha-māsikā-vacano'nunāsikaḥ*.

88. *Ibid.*, I.2.27: *ukālo'j hrasva-dīrgha-plutaḥ*.

89. *Ibid.*, VIII. 4.1.

get *ṛ* as a cerebral sound. According to the *Pāṇinīya-Śikṣā,* (11) too, *ṛ* as well as *ṣ* is a cerebral sound (Prātiśākhyas have *ṛ* either in the roots of the teeth or close to the teeth).[90]

In order to ascertain the dates of composition of the two texts, *Pāṇinīya-Śikṣā* and *Aṣṭādhyāyī,* we must trace the various types of Śikṣā, as mentioned in the *Taittirīya Upaniṣad,* i.e., *varṇa, svara, mātrā, bala, sāma,* and *santāna.* Pāṇini has treated *svara, mātrā* and *santāna* (*saṁhitā*) in his grammar. Of the remaining three branches, *bala* and *sāma* can scarely be the fit subject of a theoretical treatise. Hence, *varṇa* (speech-sounds) alone was left without treatment in the *Aṣṭādhyāyī.* Pāṇini formulated his great *Śabdānuśāsana,* the *Vyākaraṇa-Vedāṅga*[91] where he missed the treatment of *varṇa.* This has been complemented by him with the composition of *Pāṇinīya-Śikṣā,* which has emerged as a companion to his famous grammar.

Pāṇini composed the *Pāṇinīya-Śikṣa* in metre and not in prose *sūtras.* The metrical style is not found in case of *Aṣṭādhyāyī,* having complex subject-matter.

The Aṣṭādhyāyī

The fundamental work of Pāṇini is the *Aṣṭādhyāyī,* the famous grammatical treatise. In the major schools of Indian grammar, second place is occupied by the scholia, called *Vārttikas,* on Pāṇinian rules by Kātyāyana. Patañjali's *Mahābhāṣya,* the work of the third of the three sages (*muni-traya*) of the most ancient period, deals both with Kātyāyana's *Vārttikas* and also, independently, with Pāṇinian statements. According to the views of G. Cardona, Paṇini's work was the object of two types of commentaries. Some commentators followed the order of rules as they appear in the *Aṣṭādhyāyī,* others

---

90. S. Varma, *op.cit.,* p. 6.

91. M. Ghosh, *op.cit.,* p. li and fn. 1.

reordered these and dealt with them in major sections concerning definitions, metarules, rules of *sandhi*, etc.

Ācārya Pāṇini compiled his own most scientific book. According to T. Goldstücker, no work struck deeper roots than his in the soil of the scientific development of India.[92] Since it contains eight *adhyāyas* (chapters), it is named as the *Aṣṭādhyāyī* or the *Aṣṭakam*. The title *Śabdānuśāsana* is also in the true tone of the subject-matter. Another name of this work is the *Vṛttisūtram*, given by Pāṇini, and which has been well explained by Pt. Mīmāṁsaka.[93] *Aṣṭādhyāyīpāṭha* is of three types, namely *prācya*, *udicya* and *dākṣiṇātya*. Some scholars[94] have classified like this on the basis of the *pūrva* Pāṇinīya and *apara* Pāṇinīya *et seq* usages of the Kāśikā.[95]

Each of the eight chapters of the *Aṣṭādhyāyī* has been divided into four quarters (*pāda*). In every quarter, the number of aphorisms is different, according to the subject-matter. Pt. Mīmāṁsaka holds that Pāṇini himself had also written the aphorism.[96] We can cite, here, the aphorisms as mentioned in the *Kāśikā*.

Aphorisms from the Kāśikā

Atha Śabdānuśāsanaṁ		1
Pratyāhāra Sūtras		14
Chapter I - 75, 73, 93, 110	=	351
Chapter II - 72, 38, 73, 85	=	268
Chapter III - 150, 188, 176, 117	=	631
Chapter IV - 178, 145, 168, 144	=	635
Chapter V - 136, 140, 119, 160	=	555

92. T. Goldstücker, "Pāṇini" vide *India, As known to Pāṇini*, p. 1.2.

93. *Sanskrit Vyākaraṇa Śāstra kā Itihāsa*, Part I, pp. 69-72 and p. 212.

94. *Ibid.*

95. *Kāśikā* on A. VI.2.104.

96. *Sanskrit Vyākaraṇa Śāstra kā Itihāsa*, part I, pp. 201-3.

Chapter VI - 223, 199, 139, 175	=	736
Chapter VII - 103, 118, 120, 97	=	438
Chapter VIII - 74, 108, 119, 68	=	369
		3998

Subject-matter of the Aṣṭādhyāyī

The first quarter of the first chapter contains *saṁjñā* and *paribhāṣā*; the second quarter of it presents *atideśa, saṁjñā, paribhāṣā* and *aśiṣya prakaraṇa*; the third quarter contains *saṁjñā, paribhāṣā* and rules for the *upagraha*;and in the fourth quarter, we find *saṁjñā*s only. The first and second quarter of the second chapter describe *samāsa*; the third quarter presents "sup" and *vibhakti*s; and the fourth quarter contains a supplement to *samāsa*s and also to *tiṅ* and *taddhitavidhi.* In the third chapter, we find *tiṅ* and *kṛt* suffixes, to be applied after roots. The fourth chapter contains *stri* suffixes and *taddhita* suffixes in some particular meanings. The fifth chapter describes *taddhita* suffixes in special meanings along with *svārthika* and *samāsānta* (post-*samāsa*) suffixes. In the first quarter of the sixth chapter, *dhātadvittva, samprasāraṇa, ātvāgamādeśa, sandhi* and *svara*; in the second quarter *samāsasvara*; in the third quarter *aluk* along with another part (*uttarapada*) *atideśa, āgama* and *dīrgha* in *saṁhitā*; and in the fourth quarter works depending on *aṅga* and *bha* are noticed. The seventh chapter presents *vikāra* and *āgamādeśa* concerned with *aṅga*. In the first quater of the eighth chapter, we find the descriptions of doubling of a word and *svara*; and in the remaining three quarters, *padavidhi, pluti* and *sandhi* are dealt with. Some scholars have pointed out a few irregularities which have been rectified by some others.[97]

Order of the Rules in Aṣṭādhyāyī

The *Aṣṭādhyāyī* is written in the forms of rules. Every *prakaraṇa*

---

97. A. Kumar, *Archaic Words in Pāṇini's Aṣṭādhyāyī*, Parimal Publications, Delhi, 1981, p. 18 and fn. 1.

of it has been arranged quite scientifically. In fact, it is too scientific to be altered. Patañjali opines that the rules in *Aṣṭādhyāyī*, very often, belong to one-syntactic-unity and that they have been stated, sporadically. Ostensibly, the arrangement of rules is for the sake of brevity in the sense that, by doing so, the *sūtrakāra* conveys some significant things by implication.[98] Bhaṭṭojī Dīkṣita in his *Siddhānta Kaumudī* had made an attempt to rearrange the rules of Pāṇini and to supply the dittoed words. But, the attempt foredoomed to failure. The *Siddhānta Kaumudī* emerged as a distinct work as difficult to follow as Pāṇini. According to Bloomfield.

> even if one restores the words that have been replaced by imaginary ditto marks, one cannot rearrange the rules in natural order, because the position of a rule is one of the features which determines its validity (with relation to apparently conflicting rules) and its order of application (with relation to other rules that apply to the same form). Other features also, such as the more or less specific character of its wording, have to be considered in deciding whether, a rule is applicable and in what relative order.[99]

From various points of view, the order of the rules in the *taddhita* section (i.e., chapters 4 and 5 of the *Aṣṭādhyāyī*) seems to be the most complicated one. The exclusion and inclusion and of *śaiṣika*-meanings in relation to certain other affixes and meanings is another intrigue in the *taddhita* section. *Adhikāra* and *anuvṛtti* are the keys to open the interlockings (done by Pāṇini) for an access to the derivational process of Pāṇini's grammar. So, they have to be indispensably grasped and carefully handled in each and every case. Fowler[100] views that

98. *Mahābhāṣya* on p. 4.1.1.

99. L. Bloomfield, "On some rules of Pāṇini" in *JAOS*, Vol. 47.

100. M. Fowler, "How arranged are Pāṇini's rules", in *JAOS*, Vol. 85, 1965.

merely by changing the order of some rules, the problem of *anuvṛtti et seq*. cannot be solved, rather it might generate into a still more complex form. Therefore, it may, only, through rewriting some *sūtra*s and then arranging them in a suitable order, be possible to think of improving upon Pāṇini's arrangement. But even then, it will not, in any way, meet and evolve with the beauty of Pāṇinian art. Bloomfield[101] observes that the basic arrangement of Pāṇini's grammar was relative to the subject-matter. Pāṇini subordinated this logical order to a requirement of conciseness: every rule is so placed that as many words as possible can be replaced by ditto marks because they repeat the words of preceding rule. Consequently, so many rules are deviated from their natural place resulting in the basic structure of the grammar, to a great extent, obscure. Worst of all, the ditto-marks (*anuvṛtti*) and their cessation (*nivṛtti*) at the end of a series of rules are not actually written in the treatise as we have it.

Several scholars have analysed the order of the rules embedded in the *Aṣṭādhyāyī*. They have studied the treatment of different grammatical classifications, *saṁjñā*s (technical feature of his description), compounds, *kāraka* relations, derivation of normal forms from verbal roots, derivation of secondary word-forms (*taddhita*s) and feminine word-forms *et seq*. In connection with the treatment of subject-matters and the order of the rules in the *Aṣṭādhyāyī*, Faddegon[102] holds that Pāṇini is wandering in a maze and the key is always missing from his hand.

Pāṇini has compressed almost the entire text in such a way that it has become one-complete-whole with almost cohesi-

---

101. L. Bloomfield, *op.cit.*

102. B. Faddegon, *Studies on Pāṇini*, Amsterdam, 1936, p. 68.

veness in the parts, viz., the rules. And this, in turn prevents the rearrangement of the rules of the *Aṣṭādhyāyī*.[103]

Nature and Style of the Aṣṭādhyāyī

Pāṇini's *Aṣṭādhyāyī* is a significant work in the history of human knowledge and activity. In the opinion of Bloomfield, "the work has been recognized as a monumental work of human intelligence."[104] According to Belvalkar, "It stands and it will always stand as long as Sanskrit continues to be studied, as a monument, at once, of encyclopedic research and technical perfection."[105] The *Aṣṭādhyāyī* is probably the oldest surviving specimen of that type of literary activity which is expressed in the aphoristic style.

Pāṇini's *Aṣṭādhyāyī* is highly technical. It can be more correctly said that the text of the *Aṣṭādhyāyī* betrays the perfection of a technical composition — a science of language. Pāṇini's treatise on grammar serves as a perenial source of research in the field of the science of language, in general, and the Sanskrit language, in particular.

Pāṇini's treatment is intelligible only with a commentary. Bloomfield[106] holds that several life-times of work will have to be spent upon Pāṇini for usable exposition of the language recorded in the *Aṣṭādhyāyī*. According to Paul Thieme[107] and some others, Pāṇini is so brief as to, often, obscure and not seldom illogical, he is so subtle as to be ambiguous and not

103. K.R. Tripathy, *Arrangement of the Rule in Pāṇini's Aṣṭādhyāyī*, Parimal Publications, Delhi, 1991, p. 5.

104. L. Bloomfield, *op.cit.*

105. S.R. Belvalkar, *Systems of Sanskrit Grammar*, Bharatiya Vidya Prakashan, Delhi, 1976.

106. L. Bloomfield, *Language*, Motilal Banarsidass, Delhi, 1964, p. 270.

107. P. Thieme, *Indian Culture*, Vol. IV, Calcutta, 1937, p. 202.

seldom incomprehensible. Bloomfield[108] opines that Pāṇini's grammar is one of the greatest monuments of man's intelligence, and not only because of the value of an accurate description of an early Indo-European Colloquial language, but also because of the great literature which uses classical Sanskrit as its medium. Pāṇini's grammar is so much condensed that it is difficult for one to follow the rules presented there. The point of the difficulty of Pāṇini's grammar is his brevity. Generally, the forms are regular. The forms become irregular if the common feature is present in only a limited number of forms — and is not a function of any definable characteristic. The irregular forms are listed by citation in the rules or as a group in the *Gaṇapāṭha*.[109]

It is indeed a fact that the old *śāstrakāra*s compiled their works in the *sūtra* style. The *Aṣṭādhyāyī* and almost all the Prātiśākhyas (except some which have been originally written in the *kārikā* form and later on those *kārikā*s were reframed into *sūtra*s) have been written into *sūtra* style and in both the works the characteristics of *sūtra*s are gleaned. There are certain rules in the *Aṣṭādhyāyī*, which are less understood due to lack of explanations. The brevity of Pāṇini's text of grammar is quite evident from its *sūtra*-style. By the *sūtra*, he tells the way of making a *pratyāhāra* (shortening). According to Burnell,[110] Pāṇini was the first man to originate this *pratyāhāra* pattern. In the *Aṣṭādhyāyī*, there are two types of *pratyāhāra*s, namely, one, grouping the letters and another, other than that. The word *anubandha* has not been used by Pāṇini in his *Aṣṭādhyāyī*. He has used a word *it*[111] in the place of *anubandha*.

---

108. L. Bloomfield, *Language*, Motilal Banarsidass, Delhi, 1964, Reprint.

109. L. Bloomfield, "On some rules of Pāṇini" in *JAOS*, Vol. 47, 1929.

110. A. Kumar, *Archaic Words in Pāṇini's Aṣṭādhyāyī*, Parimal Publications, Delhi, 1981, p. 23 and fn. 4.

111. *Aṣṭādhyāyī*, I.3.2.

Cāndravṛtti admits that the word *it* is true to the sense.[112] Macdonell opines that *it* is the compressed form of the word *iti* and, hence, stands symbolical for the word *iti*.[113] Ostensibly, the introduction of *anubandhas* has not been originated by Pāṇini; rather he gave a new style to it.[114] The use of *anubandhas* was frequent and in an advanced stage during the time of the *Mahābhāṣya*.[115] This style of employing *anubandhas* is marked in the *Vājasaneyī Prātiśākhya* also at various places.[116]

Following the *śāstras*, the *Aṣṭādhyāyī* and the Prātiśākhyas have made use of a number of *saṁjñās* and *paribhāṣās* for the sake of brevity and clarification. Another component of the *śāstras* is the *gaṇapāṭha*. *Gaṇa* means a group. Grammarians selected a group of words which were similarly to be dealt with. A name was assigned to the first word and then the other words of the group were followed by using *ādi* to it. By doing this, the tedious job of counting and naming all the words could be avoided. Acārya Pāṇini has used 222 *gaṇas* in his *Aṣṭādhyāyī*. This style of employing *gaṇas* is a speciality of Pāṇini and not of the writers of the Prātiśākhyas except the anthor of *Vājasaneyī Prātiśākhya*, who was acquainted with the way of using *gaṇas*.[117]

In the *Aṣṭādhyāyī*, the style of using *nipātana* is also observed. *Nipātana* gives the special meaning of a word characteristic of an Ācārya. Kaiyaṭa[118] finds some difference between a *vidhi* and a *nipātana*. This difference is — where

112. *Cāndravṛtti*, 1.1.5.

113. A. Kumar, *op.cit.*, p. 25 and fn. 1.

114. Cf. A.C. Burnell, "The invention of a new system of anubandhas", on the *Aindra*, p. 39.

115. *Mahābhāṣya*, 4.2.45.

116. A. Kumar, *op.cit.*, p. 26.

117. *Vājasaneyī Prātiśākhya*, V.38.

118. Kaiyaṭa, *AV*, 1.59 (*Pradīpa*) Also, cf. A. Kumar, *op.cit.*, p. 32.

parts of a word are shown and the word is to be inferred, that is *vidhi* and where a word is seen and its parts are to be inferred, that is *nipātana*. The other feature of the *Aṣṭādhyāyī* is *adhikāra* (*anuvṛtti*) which means *viniyoga*,[119] i.e., placement of an aphorism or a part of it with the other aphorism. Such a process joins one another like a thread. Including Pāṇini, other grammarians have also used various words and expressions to denote the limit of an *adhikāra*. Under this head, we have *prāk, ca, āṅ, et seq*.

Date of Pāṇini

The majority of scholars agrees that Pāṇini flourished in 500 BC. Renou[120] opined that Pāṇini's date was either the fourth century BC or the fifth century BC. Thieme[121] suggested that Pāṇini's date certainly was earlier than the fourth century BC and, probably, not later than, fifth century BC. Similarly, V.S. Agrawala[122] placed Pāṇini at about 500 BC, and S. Bhattacharya[123] also put him at not later than the sixth century BC. In the view of Charpentier,[124] the date of Pāṇini is not later than the second half of the sixth century BC. This date was drawn by him basing on the argument that Pāṇini's rule 4.1.175 which shows he must have known of a Kāmboja king. K.B. Pathak[125] claimed the date of Pāṇini as seventh century BC and S.K.

119. *Kāśikā*, I.3.11.

120. Cf. G. Cardona, *Pāṇini — A Survey of Research*, p. 260.

121. P. Thieme, "Linguistic Sciences", *India, Pakistan, Ceylon*, ed. W.N. Brown, Philadelphia, University of Pennsylvania Press, pp. 72-74.

122. V.S. Agrawala, *India as known to Pāṇini*, Pṛthivī Prakashan, Varanasi, 1963, p. 478.

123. S. Bhattacharya, "A Note on Paṇini", *Bharati*, 6, 1963, pp. 76-80.

124. J. Charpentier, "The name Kambyses," *ZII*, 2, 1923, pp. 140-52.

125. K.B. Pathak, "The age of Pāṇini and Sanskrit as a spoken language," *ABORI*, 11, 1930, pp. 59-83.

Belvalkar[126] placed him between seventh and sixth century BC. On the other hand, V.N. Gokhale[127] drew the date of Pāṇini between sixth and fifth century BC before the Buddha. Considering all these, George Cardona[128] concludes that the most competent scholars have favoured placing Pāṇini at a time, earlier than the fourth century BC.

Some other scholars, like, Winternitz,[129] S.K. Chatterji,[130] Macdonell[131] Liebich,[132] Keith[133] and Goldstücker,[134] had tried to place Pāṇini at about 350 BC. Their main argument against an earlier date is the fact that Pāṇini used the word *yavana* which, they think, could not have entered India before Alexander's invasion. But this argument has been very ably refuted by professors S.K. Belvalkar[135] and H. Sköld.[136] Prof. Liebich[137] has proved that Pāṇini's rules apply to the language of the *Brāhmaṇas*, some obsolete (papers archaic) forms only

126. S.K. Belvalkar, *An account of the different existing systems of Sanskrit grammar*, being the Vishwanath Narayan Mandlik gold medal prize essay for 1909, Poona, The author, 1915, p. 15.
127. V.N. Gokhale, "Studies in Pāṇini, Part II: Some thoughts on Pāṇini's grammar," *PO*, 5, 1940, pp. 109-22.
128. G. Cardona, *Pāṇini — A Survey of Research*, Motilal Banarsidass, Delhi, 1980, p. 260.
129. M. Winternitz, *History of Indian Literature*, Vol. III, pp. 883 f.
130. S.K. Chatterji, *Origin and Development of the Bengali Language*, pp. 96, 31f.
131. A.A. Macdonell, *India's Past*, Oxford, 1927, p. 136.
132. B. Liebich, *Pāṇini*, Leipzig, 1891., p. 8.
133. A.B. Keith, *Harvad Oriental Series*, Vol. 18, pp. clxviii f.
134. T. Goldstücker, *Pāṇini, his place in Sanskrit literature*, Trübner, London, 1861 (Reprint: The Pāṇini Office, Allahabad, 1914).
135. S.K. Belvalkar, *Systems of Sanskrit Grammar*, Poona, 1915, pp. 15ff.
136. H. Sköld, *Papers on Pāṇini*, London, 1926, pp. 24 ff.
137. B. Liebich, *Pāṇini*, Leipzig, 1891, p. 38.

separating his language from that of the *Brāhmaṇas*. Following Prof. Liebich, Prof. Sköld thinks that Pāṇini must have belonged to the latter Vedic period of the Indian literature, probably, a period shortly preceding the *sūtra* literature proper. Now, the *sūtra* works which are considered to be among the oldest have been placed at 500 BC.[138] Thus, it seems that Pāṇini flourished sometime before 500 BC and, in no case, later than this.

The first great ancillary work to Pāṇini's grammar is the *Mahābhāṣya* of Patañjali. In this treatise, Patañjali discusses the supplementary aphorisms (*vārttikas*) of his predecessor Kātyāyana, which justify the rules of Pāṇini. Patañjali gives the critique of Kātyāyana's *vāttikas* deciding for or against each one, and adds *vārttikas* of his own.

Kātyāyana's Grammar

Kātyāyana did not himself receive the grammar, directly, from Pāṇini. He, too, had to interpret the meaning and intention of rules.[139] Besides, Kātyāyana was aware of his predecessors who had subjected Pāṇini's rules to the same kind of scrutiny as his.[140] According to Goldstücker[141] and Weber,[142] Kātyāyana was an eastern grammarian. But, R.G. Bhandarkar[143] dis-

---

138. A.A. Macdonell, *India's Past*, Oxford, 1927, p. 136.

139. P. Thieme, *Pāṇini and the Veda, Studies in the early history of linguistic Science in India*, Globe press, Allahabad, p. 130

140. L.F. Kielhorn, "Notes on the Mahābhāṣya, 5, the authorities on grammar quoted in the Mahābhāṣya," *IA* 16, 1887, pp. 101-06.

141. T. Goldstücker, *Pāṇini, his Place in Sanskrit Literature*, London, Trübner, 1861, pp. 217, 236.

142. A. Weber, "Zur Frage über das Zeitaller Pāṇinis, mit specieller Beziehung auf Th. Goldstückers 'prefare' zum 'Mānavakalpasūtra'," *Indische Studien* 5, Lesipzig, 1862, p. 44.

143. R.G. Bhandarkar, *Patañjali's Mahāvāṣya, Indian Antiquary*, 2, Bombay 1873, pp. 69-71 and Reprint under the title *Mahābhāṣya of Patañjali*, 1927-33, 1, pp. 123-24.

covered that Kātyāyana was a southerner. This fact was evident from the use of the phrase *yathā laukika-vaidikeṣu*. The term *laukika-vaidika* is composed of items containing *taddhita* affixes and, hence, Patañjali says that the southerners are fond of items containing *taddhita* affixes. Modern scholars have accepted this view explicitly.[144]

Belvalkar[145] said of Kātyāyana that ". . . his object was not to explain Pāṇini but to find fault in his grammar." More recently, Vidya Niwas Misra[146] has also accepted the view that one of Kātyāyana's purpose was ". . . to doubt the validity of the rules of Pāṇini with reference to the language in use in his time and era" and cited Goldstücker as a reference.[147]

Kātyāyana somehow belonged to a different school of grammar than did Pāṇini and Patañjali. According to Belvalkar,[148] Kātyāyana used terms such as *svara* 'vowel' in addition to Pāṇinian terms such as *ac* 'vowel'. Further, a story in the *Kathā-sarit-sāgara* (twelfth century) makes Kātyāyana a follower of an earlier school of grammar and this indicates that, most probably, he belonged to a school of grammar different from Pāṇini's.[149] This is none other than the Aindra school. Other scholars also maintain that Kātyayana followed the Aindra school as opposed to Pāṇini, who was an adherent

---

144. G. Cardona, *Pāṇini: A Survey of Research*, MLBD, Delhi, 1980, p. 269.
145. S.K. Belvalkar, *An account of the different exiting systems of Sanskrit grammar*, Poona, 1915, p. 29.
146. V.N. Misr, *The descriptive technique of Pāṇini, An introduction, Janua Linguarum, Series practica*, 18, The Hague-Paris, Mouton, 1966, pp. 25-26.
147. G. Cardona, *Review of Vidya Niwas Misra* (1966), Lg. 44, p. 647.
148. S.K. Belvalkar, *op.cit.*, 1915, pp. 30-31.
149. Vedapati Mishra, *Vyākaraṇa Vārttika — eka Samīkṣātmaka adhyayana*, Pṛthivī Prakashan, Varanasi, 1970, pp. 60, 68.

of the Māheśvara school. Vidya Niwas Misra[150] points out that Kātyāyana could not understand properly the real significance of the definitional terms in Pāṇini. George Cardona[151] thinks that the above claim remains unsubstantiated. S.D. Joshi[152] observed that Kātyāyana was an adherent of a school other than Pāṇini's. According to Joshi, Kātyāyana's views were more philosophical.[153] Earlier K. Madhava Krishna Sarma conceived the same view contrasting Kātyāyana, the theorist, with Patañjali. Ostensibly, Kātyāyana's grammar is away from unnecessary theorization.

Goldstücker[155] discovered that grammatical forms current at Pāṇini's time became obsolete by Kātyāyana's time developing different meanings of the words. R.G. Bhandarkar,[156] along with some other scholars noted that changes occurred in Sanskrit between the times of Pāṇini and Kātyāyana such as that the latter introduced additional statements to account for the derivation of new forms. In this connection, we can cite the following example. Pāṇini[157] directly provides for the use of *kṛ* (do, make) in periphrastic perfect forms of the type *īhāṁcakre* (desired, strove). However, the verbs as *bhū* (be) also occur in this formation; for example, *āmantrayāmāsa*

150. Vidya Niwas Misra, *The descriptive technique of Pāṇini, An introduction*, *JLSP*, 18, The Hagne-Paris, Mouton, 1966, p. 25.

151. G. Cardona, *op.cit.*, p. 251.

152. S.D. Joshi, *Patañjali's Vyākaraṇa-mahābhāṣya Samarthāhnika*, Edited with translation and explanatory notes, University of Poona, Poona, 1968, p. xvi.

153. *Ibid.*

154. K.M.K. Sarma, "Technical terms in the Aṣṭādhyāyī," *JOR*, 14, p. 204.

155. T. Goldstücker, *Pāṇini, his place in Sanskrit Literature*, Trübner, London, 1861, pp. 122-28.

156. R.G. Bhandarkar, "Development of language and of Sanskrit," *JBBRAS*, 16, pp. 267-70.

157. *Aṣṭādhyāyī*, 3.1.40.

(invited). Kātyāyana[158] declares that the use of all three verbs is to be accounted for in the periphrastic derivation and Patañjali shows how Pāṇini's rule can be interpreted to provide this. *Kṛ* is considered an abbreviation by Kielhorn.[159] According to Thieme,[160] both Kātyāyana and Patañjali look upon Pāṇini's grammar as a code containing the laws of correct word formation and make the assumption that this code must be valid for all times to come. Devasthali[161] opines that the aim of Kātyāyana (and even of Patañjali) in composing their works must have been not to correct him (Pāṇini), but to supplement him in view of the changes that had occurred in Sanskrit. This is also the view of Laddu.[162] Earlier, S.P. Chaturvedi opined that Kātyāyana never lost touch with the changing aspect of the language.[163] Rocher herself accepts that Kātyāyana has suggested additions to the grammar and such additions account for newer forms.[164] George Cardona holds that such linguistic changes cannot be made to account for all or even most of Kātyāyana's *vārttikas*.[165] Kātyāyana was aware of the need to account for forms which were, historically, posterior to Pāṇini.

---

158. *Vārttika* 3; 3.1.40.
159. L.F. Kielhorn, "Notes on the Mahābhāṣya; 7: Some devices of Indian grammarians", *IA*, 16, p. 248.
160. P. Thieme, "Pāṇini and the Pāṇinīyas", *JAOS*, 76, 1956, p. 22.
161. G.V. Devasthali, "The aim of the *Vārttikas* of Kātyāyana", *Festschrift K.M. Munshi*, 1960-61, Issued 1968, pp. 57-58.
162. S.D. Laddu, "Kātyāyana's *Vārttika* on Pāṇini 3.1.133 and its bearing on the text of the Mahābhāṣya", *VIJ*, 4, 1966, pp. 14-18.
163. S.P. Chaturvedi, "Scholastic disquisitions in the Pāṇinian system of grammar", *Bhārtīya Vidya*, Bombay, 1940, p. 60.
164. R. Rocher, *La Thèorie des voix du verbe dans l'ecole Pāṇineenne (le 14e āhnika)*, Presses Universitaires de Bruxeller, 1968, p. 277.
165. G. Cardona, *Pāṇini: A Survey of Research*, MLBD, Delhi, 1980, p. 253.

Kātyāyana, like, later, Pāṇinīyas, recognized that there were different kinds of objects (*karman*). This distinction was not considered pertinent by Pāṇini in stating rule 3.2.1.[166] Katyāyana and Patañjali make use not only of metarules which were not directly stated by Pāṇini but also of general techniques of interpretation. Kielhorn[167] had drawn the summary of this and, later, Renou[168] had treated this extensively.

Date of Kātyāyana

Kātyāyana's date is still in illusion. Much evidences are not available for ascertaining the date of Kātyāyana. According to Lévi,[169] Kātyayana is a contemporary of Alexander, the Great. From the term *devānāṁ-priya*, Lévi drew his conclusion. Scharfe[170] suggests that the term *devānāṁ-priya* is a court-title meaning "friend of the kings."[171] George Cardona's view also favours this.[172] According to Scharfe, the term *śāka-pārthiva* "king who eats vegetables" was used by Kātyāyana to refer to king Aśoka, so that Kātyāyana is to be placed in the middle

166. *Ibid.*, p. 255 and fn. 374.

167. L.F. Kielhorn, Notes on the Mahābhāṣya; 7. Some devices of Indian grammarians", *IA*, 16, pp. 244-52.

168. L. Renou, La Durghaṭavṛtti de Śaraṇadeva, traité grammatical en Sanskrit du xiie Siécle, édité et traduit; tome 1, fascicule I: Introduction — quoted in G. Cardona's *Pāṇini: A Survey of Research, op.cit.*, p. 254.

169. S. Lévi, "Notes de chronologie indienne; *devānāṁpriya*; Aśoka et Kātyāyana", *JAS*, 1891, pp. 549-53.

170. H. Scharfe, "The Maurya dynasty and the Seleucids," *KZ* 85, 1971, pp. 215.

171. *Ibid.*, p. 224.

172. G. Cardona, *Pāṇini: A Survey of Research*, MLBD, Delhi, 1980, p. 267.

of the third century BC. Jayapāla Vidyālaṅkāra[173] also puts Kātyāyana at about 250 BC.

Interpreting the compound *śāka-pārthiva* as meaning "Pārthivas who are Śākas," K.P. Jayaswal[174] placed Kātyāyana in between 248 to 180 BC. But, Jayapāla Vidyālaṅkāra's view is acceptable on the ground that Jayaswal's interpretation is not appropriate to Kātyāyana's *Vārttika*.[175]

There is a time-gap between Pāṇini and Kātyāyana, because the latter did not himself receive the grammar, directly, from Pāṇini. He too had to interpret the meaning and intention of rules.[176] Kielhorn[177] opines that Kātyāyana was aware of his predecessors who had subjected Pāṇini's rules to the same kind of scrutiny as their own. Since the language of Kātyāyana's time and place is different from that of Pāṇini's, there exists a time interval between the two. It is also observed that between Kātyāyana and Patañjali there intervened grammarians who composed *Vārttikas* and interpreted Kātyāyana's statements.[178]

Patañali's Grammar

Patañjali wrote his *Mahābhāṣya* in 200 BC, preserving the *Vārttika*s of Kātyāyana. The *Mahābhāṣya*, as the name itself indicates, is a voluminous work, written on the *Vārttika*s and a number of

173. J. Vidyālaṅkāra,"Kātyāyana ke Kāla-nirdhāraṇa meṁ devānāṁ-priya śabda kā mahattva," *JDSDU*, 1.2, 1972, p. 121.

174. K.P. Jayaswal, "Dates of Pāṇini and Kātyāyāna," *IA*, 47, 1918, p. 138. Also, "Kātyāyana and Pārthiva," *IA*, 48, 1919, p. 12.

175. G. Cardona, *op.cit.*, p. 267 and fn. 411.

176. P. Thieme, *Pāṇini and the Veda; Studies in the early history of linguistic science in India*, Globe Press, Aliahabad, 1935, p. 130.

177. L.F. Kielhorn, "Notes on the Mahābhāshya; 5. the authorities on grammar quoted in the Mahābhāṣya," *IA*, 16, pp. 103-4.

178. *Ibid.*, pp. 104-06.

sūtras of the *Aṣṭādhyāyī*. In the *Mahābhāṣya*, Patañjali records the earliest discussion on Sanskrit language and grammar between Bṛhaspati, the teacher and Indra, the taught. The correct and intended meanings of the Pāṇinian *sūtras* have been presented in the *Mahābhāṣya* in a scholarly way. The presentation is simple and the style is lucid. R.S. Saini holds that the opinion, expressed by Patañjali regarding many debatable grammatical issues, has been accepted as the last and final word in the subsequent grammatical works.[179] It is also observed that the *vyākaraṇa* presented in the *Aṣṭādhyāyī* by Pāṇini found its culmination in the *Mahābhāṣya*. The three works, namely the *Aṣṭādhyāyī* of Pāṇini, the *Vārttikas* of Kātyāyana and the *Mahābhāṣya* of Patañjali, collectively, came to be regarded in high esteem as *Trimuni-Vyākaraṇam*. Prof. K.V. Abhyankar has compared the work of Patañjali with *Ākara*. The *Mahābhāṣya* is, no doubt, an encyclopaedic one. According to Abhyankar, the work is spread over such a wide field of grammatical studies that not a single grammatical issue appears to have been left out.[180]

Patañjali felt the need of an explanation (*vyākhyāna*) of rules in the case of a grammar. According to him,[181] such *vyākhyāna* consisted of the following: an analysis of a rule into its components, suppletion of items necessary to the understanding of the rule, citation of examples (*udāharaṇa*) and counter-examples (*pratyudāharaṇa*), illustrating how the rule operates. It is most probable that Patañjali was aware of the commentaries on the *Aṣṭādhyāyī*. A brief survey of the

179. R.S. Saini, *Post-Pāṇinian Systems of Sanskrit Grammar*, Parimal Publications, Delhi, 1999, p. 7.

180. K.V. Abhyankar, *A Dictionary of Sanskrit Grammar*, Baroda, 1961.

181. L.F. Kielhorn (ed.), *The Vyākaraṇa-Mahābhāṣya of Patañjali*, Vol. I, Government Central Press, Bombay, 1980, 11, pp. 22-23; 12, pp. 24-26.

authorities has been mentioned in the *Mahābhāṣya*.[182] Pāṇinian commentators themselves refer to commentaries, some of which are considered to predate Patañjali.[183] R.S. Bhattacharya has also discussed on the characteristics of a *vṛtti*.[184]

Patañjali appears to have made a close study of the method and explanations of the *sūtra*s of Pāṇini, given at various academies all over the country and incorporated the gist of those studies, given in the form of *vārttika*s at the various places, in his great work. He has thoroughly scrutinized and commented upon the *vārttika*s, many of which he has approved, some of which he has rejected, and a few of which he has supplemented. Besides the *vārttika*s, he has quoted stanzas which verily sum up the arguments in explanation of the difficult *sūtra*s, composed by his predecessors.[185]

Mahābhāṣya

Kielhorn's edition (1880-85) of the text alone of the *Mahābhāṣya* is a standard one. This has been re-edited by K.V. Abhyankar (1962-72), who has added some notes, entered accents where these are pertinent to the discussions, and cited the text of rules where Kielhorn had earlier given only the number of

---

182. L.F. Kielhorn, "*Notes on the Mahābhāṣya* : 5. The authorities on grammar quoted in the Mahābhāṣya," *IA*, 16, pp. 101-6.

183. S.C. Chakravarti, *The Kāśikā Vivaraṇa Pañjikā* (the *Nyāsa*), a commentary on Vāmana-Jayāditya's Kāśikā by Jitendra Buddhi; Edited with introduction and occasional notes (*Kāśikā-vivaraṇa-Pañjikā, bodhisattva-deśiyācārya-jitendra buddhipāda-viracita*) The Varendra Research Society, Rajshahi, 1919-25, Vol.I, Introduction pp. 8-9.

184. K.S. Bhattacharya, "Kinds of exposition in Sanskrit Literature," *ABORI*, 36, 1955, pp. 124-26.

185. R.S. Saini, *Post-Paṇinian Systems of Sanskrit Grammar*, Parimal Publications, Delhi, 1999, p. 7.

each rule referred to but not directly cited in the course of a discussion.[186]

The entire *Mahābhāṣya* is divided into 85 sections which are given the name of lesson or *ānhika*. Probably, the author might have intended that the subject-matter of each lesson, was to be studied in one day each, subject to the pre-conditions that the student has already made a thorough study of the subject and is very sharp in intelligence.[187]

Time and again, Patañjali talks of *laukika* words and Vedic words which justify the correctness of a word on the basis of its "usage" in the world (*lokaṭaḥ pramāṇam*). It is true that Patañjali was very much aware of the vernaculars of that time. Ostensibly, he was able to preserve Sanskrit as per the Pāṇinian rules. Therefore, the *Mahābhāṣya* is considered a store-house of information about ancient India in all the matters, including political, economical, social, literary, philosophical and scientific.

Out of a number of commentaries and sub-commentaries of the *Mahabhāṣya*, only a few are available. Pt. Yudhiṣṭhira Mīmāṁsaka, in his work, *Sanskrit Vyākaraṇa Śāstra kā Itihāsa*, (Vol. I) has mentioned the details of those grammarians along with the names of the books, as composed by them, concerning the *Mahābhāṣya*.[188] The two major commentaries on the *Mahābhāṣya*, preserved in full, are the *Mahābhāṣya-pradīpa* or simply the *Pradīpa* by Kaiyaṭa (early eleventh century) and the *Mahā-bhāṣya-pradīpoddyota* or simply *Uddyota* by Nāgeśabhaṭṭa. The latter is in the first instance, a commentary on the *Pradīpa* but Nāgeśa, often, differs from Kaiyaṭa and offers, what he considers, the proper interpretation of a

186. G. Cardona, *Pāṇini: A Survey of Research*, MLBD, Delhi, 1980, p. 244.

187. R.S. Saini, *op.cit.*, p. 8.

188. *Ibid.*, p. 9.

Mahābhāṣya passage. It is to be noted, here, that the present text of the *Mahābhāṣya* is based upon the text procured and preserved by Candrācārya, a Bauddhist *saṁnyāsī*, who was the teacher of king Abhimanyu of Kashmir in AD, 500 century as per the evidence traced in the *Mahābhāṣya-Dīpikā* of Bhartṛhari.

yaḥ patañjaliśiṣyebhyo bhraṣṭo vyākaraṇagamaḥ,
kāle saḥ dākṣiṇātveṣu granthamātre vyavasthitaḥ ।
parvatādāgamaṁ labdhvā bhāṣyabījānusārbhiḥ,
sa nīto bahuśakhatvaṁ candrācāryādibhiḥ punaḥ ॥
— *Vākyapadīya*, II. 488-89

There is only one complete translation of the *Mahābhāṣya*, the Marāṭhī translation by V.S. Abhyankar, edited by his son.[189] This includes also the text of the *Mahābhāṣya* and notes.

A complete word-index to the *Mahābhāṣya* with references to pages and lines of Kielhorn's edition is also available. This is compiled by Pathak and Chitrao.[190] The *Mahābhāṣya* contains also *vārttika*-like statements in verse-form, called *śloka-vārttikas*.[191] Various authors like Goldstücker, Kielhorn, Bhārgavaśāstrī Joshi and Vedapati Mishra have discussed on some of these *śloka-vārttikas*.[192] They have opined that these *vārttikas* belong to the works of different authors, including those of Kātyāyana and Patañjali.

189. V.S. Abhyankar and K.V. Abhyankar, *Patañjali's Vyākaraṇa-Mahābhāṣya;* Sanskrit text and Marathi translation by Vāsudeva Śastri Abhyankar, edited by K.V. Abhyankar, 7 Vols., Deccan Education Society, Poona, 1938-54.

190. S.S. Pathak, and S.S. Chitrao, *Word Index to Patañjali's Vyākaraṇa Mahābhāṣya* (*Mahābhāṣya-śabdakośaḥ*) (= GovOS-C 1), BORI, Poona, 1927.

191. G. Cardona, *op.cit.*, p. 247 and fn. 351.

192. *Ibid.*

The *Mahābhāṣya* is composed in the form of dialogues in which both the teacher (*ācārya*) and the taught (*śiṣya*) have taken part. In the course of discussion, an unaccomplished teacher (*ācāryadeśīya*) suggests solutions to the questions raised by the student regarding the purpose of rules. As these suggestions are not fully acceptable, a teacher (*ācārya*) states the finally acceptable view (*siddhānta*). The argumentation involved in these discussions includes the citation of examples (*udāharaṇa*) and counter-examples (*pratyudāharaṇa*) for rules and also illustration (*dṛṣṭānta*), showing how things proceed in grammar, in some ways, parallel to real life.[193]

It is not always easy to arrive at a real *siddhānta* because Patañjali commonly presents arguments to support or reject several views. One is left to infer what is the true *siddhānta*.

Date of Patañjali

Patañjali's date has been fixed following evidences collected from the *Mahābhāṣya*. Basing on the analysis of the rule 5.3.99 (*jīvikārthe cāpaṇye*), Goldstücker[194] has established that Patañjali post-dated the Maurya king, Candragupta Maurya and, hence flourished later than 315 BC.[195] Again, Goldstücker, following the rule 3.2.111 (*anadyatane laṅ*), has concluded that Patañjali wrote his comments on this rule between 140 and 120 BC.[196] Analysing rule 3.2.123 (*vartamāne laṭ*), on the basis of Kātyāyana's *Vārttika*, R.G. Bhandarkar shows that Puṣyamitra, the beginner of the Śuṅga dynasty, was having a sacrifice performed at the time of Patañjali. Therefore, Patañjali's date

193. *Ibid.*, p. 253.

194. T. Goldstücker, *Pāṇini, His place in Sanskrit Literature*, Trübner, London, 1861, pp. 228-29, Reprinted by The Pāṇini Office, Allahabad, 1914.

195. G. Cardona, *op.cit.*, p. 263 & fn. 396.

196. *Ibid.*, p. 263 & fn. 399.

is set at between 178 and 142 BC.[197] The following three examples

(i) *aruṇad yavanaḥ sāketaṁ* (the Yavana besieged Sāketa)

(ii) *aruṇad yavano madhyamikām* (the Yavana besieged Mādhyamika)

(iii) *iha puṣyamitraṁ yājayāmaḥ* (we are officiating here at Puṣyamitra's sacrifice)

used by Patañjali are forced to much debate by the scholars. Weber, interpreting the example (ii), concluded that the date of Patañjali falls between AD 5 and 45. After Bhandarkar's paper[198] appeared, Weber[199] replied, placing Patañjali at AD 25. Liebich accepted that the examples (i) and (ii) were indeed Patañjali's own, so that his date could be set at *ca.* 150 BC.[200] Other scholars like V. Smith,[201] Ramaprasad Chandra,[202] Haraprasāda Śāstrī,[203] V.S. Agrawala[204] and Yudhiṣṭhira

---

197. *Ibid.*, p. 264.

198. R.G. Bhandarkar, "On the date of Patañjali and the king in whose reign he lived," *IA*, 1, 1872, pp. 299-302.

199. A. Weber, "Remarks on parts X and X1," *IA*, 2; 1873, pp. 57-59.

200. B. Liebich, *Kṣīrataraṅgiṇī, Kṣīrasvāmin's Kommentar Zu Pāṇini's Dhātupāṭha, Zum, eastern Mal herausgegeben; mit fünf Anhāngen* (=*Indf* Doppelheft 8/9), Marcus, Breslau, 1930, pp. 264-65.

201. V.A. Smith, *The early history of India from 600* BC *to the Muhammedan conquest, including the invasion of Alexander, the Great*, Clarendon Press, Oxford, 1954, pp. 227-29.

202. Ramaprasad Chandra, "Puṣyamitra and the Śuṅga empire," *IHQ*, 5, 1929, pp. 393-407, 587-613.

203. H. Śāstrī, *A descriptive Catalogue of the Sanskrit manuscripts in the collections of the Asiatic Society of Bengal; Volume 6: Vyākaraṇa Manuscripts*, Asiatic Society of Bengal, Calcutta, 1931, p. xxii.

204. V.S. Agrawala, "A note on puṣyamānava," *JOIB*, 6; 1956-57, pp. 109-10.

Mīmāṁsaka[205] also hold the same view. Still, C. Kunhan Raja[206] expressed doubts:

> We have to yet ascertain whether he (Patañjali) gave the examples *aruṇad yavanaḥ sāketam* . . . as a contemporary event, as his own sentence, or whether he took it from any record that was contemporaneous with the event.

Moreover, Frauwallner[207] again said that Patañjali could have taken example (ii) from some source. The *Kāśikā* on 3.2.111 repeats the *Mahābhāṣya* examples. According to George Cardona,[208] the examples (i), (ii) and (iii) actually belonged to Patañjali.

Other arguments have been made against placing Patañjali in the middle of the second century BC. Peterson has tried to place Patañjali from the fourth to fifth century AD. But, R.G. Bhandarkar has countered, effectively, the opinion of Peterson.[209] On the basis of Pāṇini's rule 2.4.10, De La Vallee Poussion[210] has suggested that Patañjali be assigned to *ca.* 50 BC. This opinion was, tentatively, accepted by Renou.[211] Analysing Patañjali's example *śaka-yavanam*, scholars like D.R. Bhandarkar, Harihar Trivedi and Konow have assigned

---

205. Yudhiṣṭhira, Mīmāṁsaka, *Saṁskṛta Vyākaraṇa-Śāstra kā itihāsa*, Rama Lal Kapar Trust, Sonepat, 1973, Vol. I, pp. 337-38.
206. C.K. Raja, Descriptive Catalogue of Sanskrit manuscripts in the Adyar Library; Volume VI, grammar, prosody and lexicography (= ALS 60), The Adyar Library, Madras, 1947, p. xvi.
207. E. Frauwallner, "Sprachtheorie und Philosophie im Mahābhāṣya des Patañjali," *WZKSOA*, 4, 1960, p. 108.
208. G. Cardona, *op cit.*, p. 265.
209. *Ibid.*
210. *Ibid.*, p. 266.
211. *Ibid.*, p. 353.

Patañjali to the second century BC.[212] Thus, the evidences, discussed above, warrant seriously to place Patañjali in the second century BC.

Place of Origin of Patañjali

Weber[213] used a statement from the *Mahābhāṣya* on 1.1.57 to show that Patañjali was an Easterner. Goldstücker[214] also tried to show that Patañjali belonged to the eastern region. According to R.G. Bhandarkar,[215] Patañjali came from an area north by north-west of Oudh (Ayodhyā).

Conclusion

Kātyāyana and Patañjali[216] note that one of the purposes of grammar is the merit (*dharma*), obtained through the knowledge, and the use of correct speech. Indeed, Pāṇinīyas consider grammar not only as a means, whereby correct usage is taught and discriminated from incorrect usage but also as a means of attaining ultimate release (*mokṣa*).[217] Obviously, the general Indian attitude towards knowledge and speech adhered to this principle. Evaluating Pāṇini's grammar from different angles, George Cardona opines that it is one of the greatest monuments of human intelligence. Kātyāyana and Patañjali make use not only of metarules which were not directly stated by Pāṇini but also of general techniques of interpretation. The *Mahābhāṣya* contains discussions of subjects on the threshold of grammar and philosophy. The Pāṇinīyas hold that the basic premise of grammar is the relation

212. G. Cardona, *op cit.*, p. 266.

213. *Ibid.*, p. 269.

214. *Ibid.*

215. *Ibid.*

216. Introductory Section of the *Mahābhāṣya*.

217. G. Cardona, *op.cit.*, p. 242.

(*sambandha*) between linguistic items (*śabda*) and their meanings (*artha*) which is fixed and permanent (*nitya*), and is not the inventions of someone. Ostensibly, the use of rule-order as a decision procedure in the grammar is not an invention of Kātyāyana or Patañjali, who merely extended the area of applications of the rules, already stated by Pāṇini. In the post-Pāṇinian systems of Sanskrit grammar, the works of Kātyāyana and Patañjali have occupied paramount positions among all other grammars, techniques, interpretations, commentaries and appendices prevailed. However, the knowledge of grammar is the shortest path for the attainment of the supreme essence of the world and is absolutely necessary for the attainment of liberation and purification of speech. Thus, the knowlege of Sanskrit Vyākaraṇa is quite indispensable and whose origin has been traced back to the times of the Vedas. The real upliftment of Sanskrit grammar started from Pāṇini and continued by Kātyāyana, Patañjali and so many other grammarians like Sarvavarmā, Candragomī, Abhayanandī, Bhojadeva, Pālyakīrti, Śākaṭāyana, Bopadeva, Ācārya Hemacandra, Anubhūtisvarūpārya, Kramadīśvara, Padmanābhadatta, Jīvagosvāmī and Rūpagosvāmī. There are also works which deal with the philosophical elements of Sanskrit Vyākaraṇa and also the language. The *Vākyapadīya* of Bhartṛhari is the earliest work representing this category.

2

Genesis of Sanskrit Grammar

Krutibas Rath

USUALLY actions are taken and policies adopted to realize envisaged goals. They are undertaken because of the strong belief in the end. In the process, the basic epistemological principles, with regard to the conception and development of Sanskrit grammar can be traced back to sheer naturalistic interpretation of the beings and the happenings in their own set-up. Observation for interpretation is totally incomplete without any prior knowledge of it. And this prior knowledge is referred to as Śruti (revelation), Smṛti (testimony) in the Vedic era. The basic epistemological principles may also be affirmed with equal warrant by different beings; even if a naturalistic analysis is adopted with equal warrants, as they vary with different; say of the weight of additional observations. They can be explained exclusively by use of empirical and logical concepts. A synthetic prior knowledge, which can be appraised ultimately by sensitive organs is the characteristic of the Indian notion of *karma*. The notion is that an individual's status is determined by his deeds (*karma*). Arguments about testimony as a source of knowledge turns partly on the question of the validity or revelation (Śruti). Related to testimony is the *pramāṇa* of analogy or *upamāna* (source of reference), logic or *vāk*. *Vāk* is placed in the *Ṛgveda* as a power of expression: the indexical sign of knowledge

(Veda) towards work (*karma*).[1] The export of these considerations, is that what constitutes a valid projection; and consequently what comes to constitute a projectable objectivity, as a result *Ṛgveda* which classifies the phenomenalistic systems: *catvāri śṛṅga, trayoasya pādā dveśīrṣi, saptahastā soasya/tridhā vadho vṛṣabho roravīti mahodevo martyāmaviveśa.*[2] Meaning: *nāma, ākhyāta, nipātana* and *visarga* are four horns; *atīta* (past), *vartamāna* (present) and *bhaviṣyata* are three feet (*kāla* or tense); *kārya* and *artha* are two heads; first to seventh inflections (*vibhakti*) are seven hands; *vakṣya, kaṇṭha* and *mūrdhā* are in touch of that lighted god *vṛṣabha*.[3] The master of voice who sounds *rirava* (sound). A linear phonetic transcription (objective value — *akṣara;* which is invariable, indestructible and perpetual in nature) is affixed with certain type of beings, as *sadajam rautimayu-rastugavo nardati charsabham/ajāvikou ca gāndhāram, krauñca vadati madhyamam/puṣpa sādhāraṇakāle kokilo rauti pañcamam/aśvastu dhaivatam rauti/niṣādam rauti kuñj-aram.*[4] For the description of aspirated syllables by different beings (elements) that the fricative palatal retroflex and dental sound (*ṣaḍaja — sa*) belongs to peacock; aspirated labial sound (*charsabha — re*) belongs to *vṛṣabha;* unaspirated voiced stops velar sound (*gāndhāra — gā*) belongs to goat; nasal labial sound (*madhyamam — mā*) belongs to crane; the unaspirated voiceless

1. *Ṛgveda. . . . . . ahameva svayamidam vadami, justam devebhirita manusebhihyam kāmaye tamtamagre kṛṇomi, tam vramhāṇam tamrusim tam sumedhām. . . . . .Vāk,* New Vedic Selection, Part 1, 5th Edn. by Telang & Chaube, Bharatiya Vidya Prakashan, Delhi, 1981, p. 213.

2. *Ṛgveda,* 3.8.10. (*Aṣṭaka* and *Varga* Division).

   Nature. . . . . .Bhāva . . . Bhāṣā-Akṣara.

3. Vināyak Mishra (Paṇḍit), *Oḍia bhāṣāra Pūra Tattva,* 1st Edn. 1965, p. 5.

4. Shreemad Amarasingh *viracita Amarakoṣa,* Edited by Haragovind Sastri, Chowkhamba Sanskrit Series Office, Vārāṇasī; 1957, p. 67.

stops labial sound (*pañcamam — pa*) belongs to cuckoo; the aspirated voiced stop dental sound (*dhaivat — dha*) belongs to house; the nasal dental sound (*nisada — ni*) belongs to elephant.

On the form and principles of the sensible and intelligible voices are publicly[5] defended in a proposed class of dissertation. The status of the concept of speeches are represented in a long standing interest as early as Vedas, arguing the proposition that speech has three dimensions and is contingent, given a different law of the effects of different substances on one another. An extension with the other properties and dimensions would have arisen. A science of all these possible kinds of speech would undoubtedly be the highest enterprise which a finite understanding could undertake in the field of language.

Nevertheless Vedas were in the areas that are not directly treated by divine revelation but that were cultivated by *Brāhmaṇas*, *Āraṇyakas* and others (*Nighaṇṭu*, *Nirukta*, etc.), although they do not seem to have been directly aquainted with Vedic versions. For example, Veda's (*Taittirīya Saṁhitā*'s) creative and conservative operations are linked to grammer (*Aindra Vyākaraṇa*) which warms all things and exercise their forces in each in accordance with the natural capacity of each. In *Taittirīya Saṁhitā*, the viewpoint is of interest, chiefly its attempt to interpret Vedic texts as a system of ritual and other injunctions which led to certain development in Vedāṅga (a logical sequence).[6] About how to consider and what to do

5. Satyavrata Sastri, *Vaidika Vyākaraṇa*, tr. from 'A Vedic Grammar for students by Arthur Anthony Macdonell, 1st Edn. Motilal Banarsidass, Delhi, 1971, p. xiii, . . . *Bhinna ruchi lokah*, i.e., Public.

6. F. Max Müller, *The Sacred Books of the East*, The Vedānta Sūtras, with commentary by Śaṅkarācārya, Translated by George Thibaut, Part II, Reprinted by Motilal Banarsidass, 1962, Oxford University Press, London, 1904, p. 220.

→

with the recital of the materials intoned in the Veda are those words, which are believed coming through the mouth of the spiritual lords.

This, too, is that he who shall act, thus, is sagacious and is the father of righteousness through wisdom and whoever would do that which has happened, thoroughly observes it on account of which it has not happened. For the aggregate and so on can be viewed there results the existence of symbols, as of nature of *akṣara Brahman* which is sublated. The sublated character is then classified into subgroups and can be viewed, as symbols to be apprehended,[7] which latter would be the case if one should take the two genitives as co-ordinate and, therefore, expressing an imaginative identification of the letter and thought. The two genitives are rather to be taken in that way that one qualifies the other.[8] It, therefore, remains a settled conclusion that *śabda* is produced from the *akṣara, Brahman,* which existed in a certain considered method. Those scriptural passages are understood in the same way as the analogous statements about the *śabda, Brahman* which has been shown to be possible. *Śabda Brahman* is modulated through ether, whose greatness is well known merely in order to indicate *akṣara Brahman*'s supereminent greatness and not in order to maintain its being equal to each other. There is no plurality of homogeneous substances, out of which the *śabda Brahman* could

---

→ p. 221, "Moreover, as the section beginning with "of him who thus knows from an *anuvāda* of some thing previously established (and as such forms one Vākya to which one sence must be ascribed) we must not bring about 'a split of the sentence' by interpreting it as teaching in the first place that . . . *Taittīrīya* text of the Vidyā".

p. 320. (44), "because scriptures declare a fruit," This is the view of Ātreya.

7. *Ibid.*, pp. 218-23, "God's capable of 'knowledge of Brahman".

8. *Ibid.*, Max Müller, pp. 221, 17.

originate. It should originate only from things belonging to the same genus, not from such as belonging to different genera. Genus is "substance," the latter to the genus' quality, the genera of essentiality, substantiality, etc. The rule would be a superfluous one; for, in that sense, every inherent cause belongs to the same genus as every other. Plurality of inherent causes, not one such cause, is able to originate an effect. The same substance when passing over into a different state as distinguished by peculiar characteristic marks, is admitted to be having an effect. It, therefore, remains a settled conclusion that before *akṣara Brahman*, *śabda Brahman* was produced and existed in Smṛti.

In the *Aṣṭādhyāyī*, Pāṇini mentions by name ten other persons all, presumably, grammarians Āpiśali, Kāśyapa, Gārgya, Gālava, Cakravarman, Bhāradvāja, Śākaṭāyana, Śākalya, Senaka and Sphoṭāyana.[9] It is proper to conclude that other grammarians, predecessors or contemporaries of Pāṇini had, like him, noted particular usages, of his own work. Moreover, evidence in the *Mahābhāṣya* of Patañjali makes us to assert that at the time of Kātyāyana and Patañjali, grammars by Āpiśali and Śākaṭāyana were known. Patañjali identifies himself as *śabda pramāṇaka*. He says we are upholders of the authority of the word; what the word says is our guide. In the *Ṛgveda*, *Brahman* is equated with language. The ultimate abode of language (*vāk*) is *Brahman*. Many Upaniṣads also elaborated the question of *Brahman* with language — *Brahman* is identified as the one reality, without a second, which is identical with language.[10] In *Māṇḍūkya Upaniṣad*, the *auṁ* is described as traversing the phenomenal level of waking,

---

9. George Cardona, *Pāṇini: A Survey of Research*, 1st Indian Reprint, Motilal Banarsidass, Delhi, 1980, p. 146.

10. *anādinidhanam brahmā sabdatattva yadākṣaram*
vivartate arthabhavena prakriyā jagato yataḥ
— *Vākyapadīya*, I. 1.

dreaming and deep sleep and as reaching out to the absolute. Some, like Pūrva-Mīmāṁsā and Vedānta, admit six methods: *pratyakṣa* (perception), *anumāna* (inference), *upamāna* (comparison), *arthāpatti* (postulation), *anupalabdhi* (non-apprehension) and *śabda* (verbality), whereas Cārvāka accepts only *pratyakṣa* as valid one. All the schools of thought do not accord independent status as a *pramāṇa*. Nyāya, Mīmāṁsā, Vedānta and Sāṅkhya are such systems which admit the validity of *śabda pramāṇa* and carry on elaborate discussions on the nature of language and its functions. For Bhartṛhari, *vāk* is not just uttered but it is an articulated speech. It is multi-layered phenomenon and uttered speech (*vaikhari*),[11] it is the final stage of the externalization of linguistic process. Before the speaker expresses himself audibly through uttered speech he has to think of the appropriate words and meanings they are supported to convey. So *vaikhari,* uttered *vāk,* presupposes a mental and pre-utterance level, i.e., *mādhyama vāk*. This, in turn, further points to a level of unity. This is the level of *paśyanti vāk*. The potent state of verbalisability is thus manifested in the form of particularized thought and intenion. In turn, this is externalized in the form of particular utterances. This way of explicating the speaker's mode of communicating meaning implies that the uttered level, along with its particularities and differentiations, actually reflects the unity

11. (i) George Cardona, *op.cit.*, pp. 242 to 251.

(ii). Bhartṛhari conceives three stages of language — the *paśyanti, madhyamā* and *vaikharī*. *Paśyanti* is the latest stage of language; there is no distinction between the word forms and meanings, so *paśyanti* is non-verbal. *Madhyamā* is intermediate stage, where despite the identity of thought and language their distinction along with the distinctive elements of words and meanings are discernible. This stage is preverbal. And *vaikharī* is the verbal stage, i.e., when the language is presented in audible form along with the elements of accent, pitch, meaning, etc. Thus, language moves from spoken words (*vaikharī*) and inner thought (*madhyamā*) to the direct mystical vision *paśyanti, pratibhā* or *sphoṭa*).

of thought and meaning. Whenever the speaker says something, he expresses as "sense" or "thought." This sense of thought is one and unitary.[12] For example, if someone intends to express that he is hungry, he would utter "I am hungry". Here, the sentence contains three words. Yet, the intention or what he means, is unitary in nature. So, for communicative purposes, the unitariness of sentence-meaning has to be assumed by the speaker though he has to express what he intends *(abhiprāya)* to say through a series of words. Yet, the "sense" expressed has a unity. A sentence-meaning may not self-complete. It is rather like the following of sentence-meaning. For example, a man living in a city, may not understand the import of the sentence *ullūko dibā na dṛśyate*, for he does not know what an *ullūka* (owl)[13] means. Here, the clarification of *ullūka* is its meaning and really the (word and meaning) have no difference at all. Then sentence is nothing but a combination of word-meanings, for there is certain completeness and unitariness about sentence-meaning. Hence, sentence-meaning is presented through individual words. They do not have any autonomy in the matter of communication of meaning. On the other hand, the problems from the hearer are likely is that he should understand the sounds, i.e., hearer's understanding (*śabdabodha*) or the sequential order of the syllable by syllable, which goes an unitary meaning by the inherent linguistic disposition (*pratibhā*). The output of sentence-meaning has been analysed and explained in a totally different way by other philosophers of languages. The *pādavādins* do not want to do away with the autonomy of words and wordmeanings. So their main concept is to analyse the basic conditions of sentence-meaning. These

12. Kālidās, *Raghuvaṁśam* — *vagarthauviva sampṛktau vagortha-upratipataye*, 1st canto, 1st stanza, *jagataḥ pitarauvande pārvatī-parameśvarau*.

13. *Ṛgveda*, X.165.4.

conditions are presumed to give a completeness and unity to sentence-meaning. The three main conditions incorporated are *ākāṅkṣā*, *yogyatā*, and *sannidhi*. Nyāya adds *tātparya* as the fourth condition in the later period. This condition is specifically meant for deciphering the contextual meaning with reference to the sentence, as a whole. But the Western approach to sentence-holism has been developed to referential-theory of meaning in the twentieth-century grammarians. And the sciences, like grammar and lexicography, concentrate on words and word-meanings, or during the linguistic expression of Sanskrit from pre-Vedic period to modern era on the basis of holistic theory of sentence-meaning in terms of semantical theory of truth (by Donald Davidson, *Truth and Meaning*), "sense" and "referent" (by Frege), use theory of meaning (by Wittgenstein), *anvitābhivāda* (by Pravakāra); pragmatics of meaning (by Grice and his followers like Schiffer, the speaker's meaning can be identified with what he is intending in a certain belief or action). However, to understand meaning in speaker's intention or the hearer's understanding is an ancient theory. It is futile to seek for the distinctive elements of semantical and psychological notations of language.[14] Grammatically, these are known parsing and analysis of words and sentences, respectively, to identify the influenced incentive behind very junction. Invariably, these favour a right cause and effect to differ from any sectarian analysis seeking the foothold of grammar, because Indian philosophy postulated that language had both phenomenal and metaphysical dimensions.

The basic work in comparing Pāṇini's rules and what they provide with the language represented in literary text was

---

14. Gayatri Rath, "Sentence individuality, Indian & Western approach", From *Vishveshharanand Indological Journal*, Vol. XXXIII-XXXIV, pts IV, Ed. Damodar Jha, Vishveshvaranand Vishva Bandhu Institute of Sanskrit & Indological Studies, Punjab University, Hosiarpur, June-Dec, 1995-96, pp. 113-26.

done by Liebich (1886-87; 1891) and was followed by Franke (1890b) and Wecker (1906). Liebich's principal conclusion was that the language, described by Pāṇini, was synthetically as good as identical with the language of the *Brāhmaṇas* and *Sūtra* texts. Pāṇini's description of how the aorist was used tallied closely with the use of the aorist in the *Aitareya Brāhmaṇa* (had earlier been pointed out by R.G. Bhandarkar).[15] According to Franke, "*bhāṣā* refers to a real language" (used in Pāṇini grammar) which is spoken language. Sanskrit of this type Pāṇini himself would not consider exemplary. "So for Pāṇini's Sanskrit", says Franke, it is really neither *bhāṣā* nor a living language. For, the *Aṣṭādhyāyī* does not teach a single organic language. Pāṇini has taken from both a living language and secondary source,[16] whereas the word is reflection, has its support from the well-known couplet *abhyāsārthe drutam vṛtim*. This state of things, as can be easily imagined, was detrimental to the purity of the Vedic culture (*brāhmaṇena na mlecchitaṁ vai*, etc.). Thus, the necessary incentive was furnished to contemporary leaders, who surely included neo-Āryans too, for studies in phonetics (*śikṣā*), metrics (*chandas*), grammar (*vyākaraṇa*) and vocabulary (*nighaṇṭu*).[17]

Prof. B. Faddegon says: Most likely the *Śiva-Sūtra* is of earlier data than the *Aṣṭādhyāyī* and the *Śiva-Sūtra* as a phonetical classification deserves the highest praise.[18] The

15. George Cardona, *Pāṇini: A Survey of Research*, 1st Indian reprint, Motilal Banarsidass, Delhi, 1980, p. 238.
16. Manmohan Ghosh, *Pāṇiniya Śikṣā*, Text and Translation, V.K. Publishing Home, New Delhi, 1991, p. xxii.
17. Prof. Lakshmana Sarup has a different opinion on this point. He is unwilling to recognize Pāṇini's grammar or *Nighaṇṭu* or similar other works as Vedāṅgas (translation & notes on the *Nighaṇṭu* and the *Nirukta*, pp. 221-23).
18. The mnemon technics of Pāṇini's Grammar, *Acta Orientalia*, VII, 1929, p. 56 and 64 respectively.

ralation of Pāṇini's technical devices to his predecessors was the dogma, i.e., the divine revelation of the *Śiva-Sūtra*. It contained as a historical nucleus. The fact is that Pāṇini did not compose the *Śiva-Sūtra* himself. Patañjali took it for granted. Pāṇini also has suggested (*jñāpayati*) the same root as *jñāpaka* (suggested or implied). To reasonably, assume is that Pāṇini might have adopted the already exitsting material (the *Śiva-Sūtra* in their original form) with certain changes as matrix of his *pratyāhāras*. And his *śikṣā* connected with his name was, perhaps, the work to which was prefixed the *varṇa-samamnāya* and furnished the basis of Pāṇini's grammar and phonetic. The relation of the *Pāṇini-Sūtra*, in its original form, may go back to the first age of the *śikṣā* Vedāṅga. According to *Taittirīya Upaniṣad* (1.2) the *śikṣā* consists of *svara* (pitch accent), *mātrā* (quality), *bala* (stress), *sama* (utterance in a medium tone); and *santāna* or *saṁhitā* (euphonic combination). In *Ṛgveda-bhāṣya*, Sāyaṇa says *sikṣā* is *varṇa svaradyucchāraṇa prakāro yatra upadiśyate sā sikṣā*. And, likewise, Pāṇini says *svaravarṇadayaḥ*, means *varṇa*, *svara*, *mātrā*, *bala*, *sama* and *santāna*. It is inferred that either Sāyaṇa was aware of Pāṇini or Pāṇini has borrowed from the concept of Vedas. But Vedic *mantras* existed, once, as an undivided corpus, because particular *mantras* are found in more Vedas than one. It hints that the *mantras* were collected under different names, chiefly, with a view to their ritual use. For example, the collection of *mantras* made for the use of *hotṛ* was called *Ṛk* and that for the use of the *adhvaryu* was called the *Yajus*, while *udgātṛ*'s collection was called the *Sāman*. Further, Vedic *mantras* by different classes were uttered differently, such as *hotṛ* recited the *Ṛks* with normal voice, the *adhvaryu* muttered the *Yajus* silently and *udgātṛ* chanted *Sāmans* loudly.[19] It must remain, probably, that in part, at least, in some hitherto unknown *śākhā*, the *Atharvaveda* exists. From these, one will easily realize the untenable nature

19. Max Müller, *op.cit.*, pp. 123-24.

of the meaning of Vedas and Vedāṅgas.

The evidences, noted and referred to, allude to one conclusion that Pāṇini indeed had predecessors in the field of grammar. What reflected in *Aṣṭādhyāyī* of Pāṇini is Āpiśali whose fulframatical treatise is not available, till now. Only the *Āpiśala-śikṣā* is attributed to Āpiśali that Pāṇini refers to.[20] *Pañcapadī* version of the *Uṇādi-Sūtras* composed by Āpiśali reasons that *Āpiśala-śikṣā* nasals appear in the order, *n, m, n, n, n,* influenced Pāṇini *Śiva-sūtra n, n, n, n, m* following the usual order of stops: velar (*k,* etc.), palatal (*c,* etc.), retroflex (*t,* etc.), dental (*t,* etc.), labial (*p,* etc). Pāṇini has to change this arrangement in order to allow (by rule 8.3.32: *namo hrasvād aci namun nityam*) sequences such as *pratynnāste* is seated facing West (*pratayan aste*). Pāṇini also mentions easteners and northerners and commentators consider that the term *udecām,* or "northerners" and *prācām* or "easterners" refer both to areas in which certain usages obtained and to schools of grammarians. However, Pāṇini's mention of other grammarians view serves to convey differences in usages and operations recognized by the grammarians. Such opinion of commentators is based on the position that Sanskrit is eternal, perennial and fixed.

Śākaṭāyana grammar was another pre-Pāṇinian grammar that Pāṇini's *Aṣṭādhyāyī* followed.[21] Another extant work, attributed by some to Śākaṭāyana, is *Ṛk-tantra* which ascribed to Audavraji. Probably, Śākaṭāyana the pre-Pāṇinian grammarian reworked on original treatise by Audavraji.[22]

---

20. Introduction to Yudhiṣṭhira Mimāṁsaka, p. 2.4, 1973.

21. Bühler (1864.703), in the course of describing the text of the Śākaṭāyan grammar had assumed that it was pre-Pāṇinian and claimed that Pāṇini's *Aṣṭādhyayī* was reworking of this treatise.

22. Geroge Cardona, *op.cit., Pāṇini,* p. 149.

Many other treatises refer to Aindra grammar that comprises a legend in *Taittirīya Saṁhitā*. According to *Taittirīya Saṁhitā vāk* was at one time undiscriminated (*avyākṛta*), the gods asked Indra to discriminate it (*vyākṛta*), which he did. Patañjali in the course of saying *Mahābhāṣya* that correct usage cannot be taught by means of a word-for-word (*pratipada*), enumeration of correct forms. So, he says: "Thus, it is handed down: Bṛhaspati proclaimed to Indra for a thousand heaven years a complete text of words listed individually and yet, he did not get to the end." "Aindra grammar is a school of grammar older than that of Pāṇinian grammar, says Burnell (1875)." It follows from the preceding enquiry that by Aindra grammar one must understand a school of grammar and not a specific work by an individual. Burnell says: "It will be seen that they really bear out this meaning and do not attribute an actual grammatical treatise to the god Indra." But critics like V.R. Ramachandra Dikshitar, Varadaraj Umarji and Prabhudayala Agnihotri have accepted Aindra grammar as a single work by Indra. For *Kātantra,* a Sanskrit grammar has been on the basis of Aindra-grammar.[23] Renou also rejects the thesis of Burnell. Moreover, Cardona concludes that Aindra-grammar is pre-Pāṇinian and identical with *Kātantra* (Sanskrit grammar).

Kāśakṛtsna is a commentator or *mahābhāṣyakāra*. Yudhiṣṭhira Mīmāṁsaka has ably collected the fragments attributed to Kāśakṛtsna and composed commentary on them. There is also a *dhātupāṭha* ascribed to Kāśakṛtsna the *Kāśakṛtsnaśabdakalāpadhātupāṭha* by A.N. Narasiṁha (Kannaḍa) and translated into Sanskrit by Yudhiṣṭhira Mīmāṁsaka. Pāṇini has borrowed *gaṇa* list from Kāsakṛtsna, says Kapil Dev Shastri.[24] Obviously, Kāśakṛtsna's *Vedānta Sūtra* commentary is Pāṇinian. The number of roots given in the *Kāśakṛtsnaśabdakalāpadhātupāṭha* is

23. *Op.cit.,* p. 151.

24. *Op.cit.,* p. 152.

greater than the number of roots in Pāṇini's *dhātupāṭha*. The general trend, in later *dhātupāṭhas*, is towards condensation. Therefore, Pāṇini's is later than Kāśakṛtsna's.

Nevertheless given the evidences, noted above, it is licit to say that Pāṇini not only had predecessors in the field of grammar but also that he built upon such previous work. Kātyāyana and Patañjali were his contemporaries. Kielhorn adopted a cautious stance, saying of Kātyāyana and Patañjali that "like Pāṇini himself, both have based their own works and have preserved in them all that was valuable in the writings of their predecessors. Some roots given in known versions of the *dhātu-paṭha* were not contained in the versions of the text received by Kātyāyana. In the fifth *vārttika*, Kātyāyana says that "a supplement is to be made to the grammar in order to include the introduction of *ṇic* to form derivative-meaning." This is to cover cases such as *sūtrayati* "makes . . . . a *sūtra*".[25] But it is a question whether the distinction between Northern and eastern grammarians that Pāṇini mentions, really existed at the time of Kātyāyana or not. According to Patañjali, Kātyāyana was a southerner.[26] In the *Mahābhāṣya*, Kātyāyana was the phrase, *yathā laukika-vaidikeṣu*, suggests two possible interpretations. Since the term, *laukika-vaidika*, is composed of items containing *taddhita* affixes, the phrase can mean as in (utterance of) worldly (usage and) Vedic (utterances, which

25. *tat karotity upasamkhyānam sūtrayatyādy artham.*

26. (i) Geroge Cardona, *op.cit.*, *Pāṇini*, pp. 268-69.

(ii) *Encyclopaedia Britannica* — "Patañjali: an ancient Indian author or authors to whom are ascribed works in Sanskrit on religions, meditation (*Yogasūtra*), grammar (*Mahābhāṣya*), medicine (*Caraka Saṁhitā*), alchemy (*Patañjala*), the Sāṅkhya philosophy (*Adhara-Kārika*), liturgical music (*Nidānasūtra*) and metrics (*Piṅgalā*, is *chhandah sūtra*) . . . discusses the grammatical aphorisms of Pāṇini and Kātyāyana's critical annotation upon them which it incorporates . . . . first and second century BC.

convey) established norms (of behaviour) (*yathā laukika vaidikeṣu ca kṛtantesu*). Patañjali also suggests that Kātyāyana has, here, used *laukika-vaidika* as equivalent to *loke vede ca* in worldly usage and in the Veda. *Priya-taddhita, dākṣiṇātyaḥ, yathāloke vede cetipra-yogktavye yathā laukikavaidikeṣu iti prayuñjate* and Bhandarkar's conclusion forwards that Renou (explicitly a modern scholar) and Yudhiṣṭhira Mīmāṁsaka take Kātyāyana as a southerner.

Patañjali was an esterner. Kāśikā and Kaiyaṭa refer to Patañjali as *ācāryadeśīya*. *Pūrvam mathurāyaḥ pāṭaliputram* concludes that Patañjali's example shows that he came from an area east of Pāṭaliputra, i.e., modern Patna. *Yo yam adhvā pāṭaliputrād gantavyas yat paraṁ sāketāt*, Pāṭaliputra or Sāketa (Ayodhyā) puts one in confusion and it is a desperate attempt to salvage rightly the place of Patañjali.[27]

The relative chronology of grammarians and their grammar treatises can be studied on the basis of Pāṇini and his creations in the light of grammar. Yāska, the author of *Nirukta* (a treatise dealing with Vedic words and their etimological explanations) has frequently been considered to antedate Pāṇini. Max-Müller takes Yāska as an earlier author than Pāṇini but has admitted the tentativeness of his statement. Goldstücker advances two evidences that (1) Pāṇini knew Yāska (Yāskādibhyogotre) and (2) Pāṇini does not define the term *upasarga* (preverb) whereas Yāska mentions various *upasarga*s and their views of use. But Liebich claims that it is wrong when both are considered on the basis of methodological differences. Thus, two groups supporting and differing the opinion of Goldstücker and Liebich put various arguments and keep that the question of priority opens foı good.[28]

27. G. Cardona, *op.cit.*, p. 27.

28. (i) *Op.cit.*, pp. 272-73.

(ii) Manmohan Ghosh, *Pāṇinīya Śikṣā*, text & translation, V.K. Publishing House, New Delhi, 1991, pp.

In the genesis of Sanskrit grammar, Prātiśākhyas came later containing accretions to older core texts. Hence, they are epigrammatically discussed that the older a *sūtra*, the more is easily it is understood and later, a *sūtra*, the less easily it is understood. According to Weber, *Vājasaneyī-Prātiśākhya* was pre-Pāṇinian. Roth, Müller, and Liebich say that the Prātiśākhyas, qua Vedic texts had to be earlier than Pāṇini. But Goldstücker and Thieme say that the Prātiśākhyas were post-Pāṇinian as they represent attempts by Kātyāyana. *Ṛk-Prātiśākhya* was composed by Śaunaka. B. Ghosh and Müller assumed that a reference to Sākalya in the *Aṣṭhādhyāyī* showed dependence on the *Ṛk-Prātiśākhya* since all, but one of the rules in the question, are not the objects of independent discussions in the *Mahābhāṣya*, they probably did not exist at the time of Patañjali. However, in spite of different opinions espoused by various critics, there is definite evidence to show that some Prātiśākhya rules were borrowed by Pāṇini's system. That the substitution procedure, adopted by Pāṇini, denoted the Prātiśākhyas. It proves that this technique is earlier than Pāṇini's substitution procedure. Further modification procedure is immediately reconcilable with morpophonemic statements of the continuous text. But this procedure is not immediately reconcilable with grammatical operations such as letting to occur in certain environments instead of as "be". So it can be concluded that all the Prātiśākhya are earlier than or posterior to Pāṇini.[29]

In the annal of post-Pāṇinian grammars, *Mahābhāṣyas*, commentaries, the *Kāśikāvṛtti*, the *Mitākṣarā*, the *Śabdakaustubha*, the *Bhāga-Vṛtti*, the *Durghaṭa-Vṛtti*.[30] *Rūpāvatāra*, the *Prakriyā-*

29. G. Cardona, *op.cit.*, pp. 274-75.

30. (i) Manmohan Ghosh, *op.cit.*, "The *pañjikā* flourished at a time when the original work of Audavraji was still available in a more or less correct form. In fact, he may be older than the *vṛttikāra* of *Ṛk-tantra* who appears by no means, to be modern. . ." →

kaumudī, the *Siddhānta-kaumudī*, commentaries on *dhātupāṭha* with the treatises on semantics and philosophy of grammar are evolved. The evidence in this matter comes from Patañjali, who, in his definition of a typical priest (*ārtvijīna-mahābhāṣyakāra*), says that he should be able to use the (Vedic) speech with (properly reflected) words, (*pada*) with (proper) accent (*svara*) and with the (properly articulated) speech-sounds (*varṇas*). Considerable effort has been developed to the realia'[31] reflected in the *Mahābhāṣya*. For Patañjali has discussed in his *Mahābhāṣya* about the geographical feature of Āryāvarta, Ābhīras, Cities, Literature of his time, Epics and other poetry, theatrical representation and grammar, etc. The *Mahābhāṣya* passages are that it concerns a shadow play (Lüders, Winternitz), a pantomime (Keith) and an actual full theatrical representation (Kane, Purī). "There were prevalent in the days of Patañjali all three representation of past events — the dramatical, the pictorial and verbal . . . ." (K.V. Abhyankar).[32]

Commentaries are not *Mahābhāṣyas*. Full commentaries are those in which all the rules are paraphrased with examples and counter examples given to illustrate their applications. Commentaries are two kinds in general, such as (1) running commentaries (as found in *Aṣṭādhyāyī*), and (2) recorded commentaries in which particular topics are brought together as in the *Aṣṭādhyāyī*, for example, the *Siddhānta-Kaumudī*.[33]

→ (ii) Ur-text of the Audavraji (but some of the other quotations in the *Pañjikā* from Audavraji are corrupt).

(iii) Kātyāyana also leans to give support as he says *vṛtti — samavāyārtha upadeśaḥ*.

31. Real things, actual facts, esp. as distinct from theories about them — Cf. *The New Shorter Oxford Eng. Dictionary on Historical Principles*, Ed. by Lesley Brown, vol. II — (N-Z), 1993 edn., p. 2493.

32. G. Cardona, *op.cit.*, p. 277.

33. G. Cardona, *op.cit.*, p. 278, *Siddhānta-Kaumudī* (See Sec. IV.3.2) →

The *Kāśikā-vṛtti* is generally referred as Kāśikā. It is an older extant complete running commentary on Pāṇini's grammar. It is the work of Jayāditya and Vāmana. As a *vṛtti*, the *Kāśikā* comments on rules by giving paraphrases which include what is to be supplied for the understanding of the rules through the application of definitions and metarules as well as through *anuvṛtti* and giving examples to illustrate how the rules apply. There are two commentaries on the *Kāśikā* : (1) *Nyāsa* by Jinendrabuddhi and (2) *Pada-mañjarī* by Haradatta. *Nyāsa* tries to show how, what is achieved through an addition to the grammar of *vārttika*, can equally be achieved by applying original rules of *vārttika*. So, no step than the *sūtra* is needed. *Pada-mañjarī* is restarted and rediscussed with extensive citations of predecessors.

Bhāṣā-vṛtti of Puruṣottamadeva is another *vṛtti*, commenting on the *Mahābhāṣya*. It is comparable to the *Kāśikā* in the method of paraphrasing rules.

The *Vyākaraṇa-mitākṣarā* is a commentary on Kaiyaṭa's *Pradīpa* in which rules are paraphrased with examples to illustrate by Annambhaṭṭa.

The *Śabda-Kaustubha* of Bhaṭṭojī Dīkṣita is an interpretation of rules of paraphrases (comparable to the Kāśikā or *Bhāṣā-vṛtti*), on the treatises of predecessors like Pāṇini, Kātyāyana, Patañjali, Bhartṛhari and his father Lakṣmīdhar. He has divided his commentaries into *āhnika*s with reference to Bhaṭṭojī. His

→ starts with a section of definition rules introducing terms (*saṁjñā prakaraṇa*), then treats major meta rules (*paribhāṣā*) and goes on to deal with: *sandhi*, operations which apply to or are conditioned by nominal endings, femine affixes, *kāraka* rules together with nominal affixation rules, compounds, *taddhita* affixation finite verb forms, derived verb roots, restricting the occurrence of verb ends (*ātmanepada* and *parasmaipada*), the meanings of L-suffixes, primary verbal affixes (*kṛttunādi* affixes, Vedic rules, accentual rules, etc.

work is syncretic, treating of views propounded by *Mahābhāṣya,* which has an introductory section called *paspaśā.* The most famous *Nyāsa* of Pāṇinian grammar after Bhartṛhari was Jinendrabuddhi whom Māgha praised. Bhaṭṭojī Dīkṣita notes that he will extract from the ocean which is the *Mahābhāṣya,* the *Kaustubha* jewel of grammar (*Śabda-Kaustubha*) and then says "grasp effortlessly from this work the meaning in its entirety which is gotten with great effort after considering many other works." Harprasad Shastri says that *Śabda-Kaustubha* is a commentary on *Mahābhāṣya* in doubt. Were it be so, one would expect Bhaṭṭojī to have commented only on those rules developed to *Mahābhāṣya,* but he could not. He was an innovator who disagrees with the great many views of Pāṇinīya. Above all, his work is a commentary on *Aṣṭādhyāyī.*[34]

The *Bhāga-vṛtti* of Vimalamati is collected from the questions, edited by Yudhiṣṭhira Mīmāṁsaka. "Vṛtti means composed", says Mīmāṁsaka. Vimalamati separates Vedic and non-Vedic rules to be considered, differently. He disagrees with Jayāditya's *Kāśikā.*

Durghaṭa-vṛtti of Śaraṇadeva is "an exposition (*vṛtti*) reconciling those *lakṣya*s (forms of words) and Pāṇini's *sūtra*s which appear difficult to reconcile (*durghaṭa*) with each other" says Gaṇapati Sastry (1909, English, Preface, p.1).

The *Rupāvatāra* is reordered commentary by the Ceylonese Buddhist Dharmakīrti. These commentaries do not treat all rules. Each section of the commentaries is called *avatāra.* The *Rūpāvatāra* has two major parts: (1) *saṁjñāvatāra* (definition rules), *saṁhitāvatāra* (*sandhi* rules), operations on and conditioned by nominal endings (*vivaktya-avatāra*), indeclinables (*avyayavatāra*), feminine affixes (*strī-pratyayavatāra*), *kāraka*

34. G. Cardona, *op.cit.*, pp. 283-84.

rules and affixation rules pertinent to them, compounds (*samāsāvatāra*) and *taddhita* affixation (*taddhitāvatāra*) and (2) *dhātu-pratyaya-pañcikā* which deals with post verbal affixes. It is like *Siddhānta-Kaumudi* but there is not Vedic and accental touch. Jaina grammarian Hemacandra quotes the *Rūpāvatāra*. It belongs to tenth or eleventh century.[35]

The *Prakriyā-Kaumudī* of Rāmacandra is the first Sanskrit commentary[36] on grammar. It does not treat all the rules of *Aṣṭadhyāyī* but contains brief section of Vedic rules, supplemented by Viṭṭhala.

The *Siddhānta-Kaumudī* is a complete *Kaumudī* work. It is the prominent *Kaumudī* in India and abroad. Bhaṭṭojī Dīkṣita has composed it (*Siddhānta-Kaumudī*) and its auto-commentary *Prauḍha-manoramā*. Both *Siddhānta-Kaumudī* and *Prauḍha-manoramā* have further been commented by *Bāla-manoramā* of Vasudeva Dīkṣita for beginners (*bāla* means child or *laghu*). Vāsudeva goes into great detail explaining derivation for beginners. The *Tattvabodhinī* of Jñānendrasarasvatī is a terser, more scholarly and demanding commentary. It is essentially a distillation of the *Prauḍha-manoramā*. But both the commentaries are not discussing the accentual and Vedic rules, on which Jayakṛṣṇa commented in his *Subodhinī* commentary on *Siddhānta-Kaumudī* has also edited by Giridhara Sarma Chaturvedi, Parameśvarānanda Sarmā Bhāskara and Gopal Shastri Nene as *Tattvabodhinī*. *Śabdenduśekhara* of Nāgeśabhaṭṭa is also a commetary in *Siddhānta-Kaumudī*. *Bṛhacchabdenduśekhara* of Sitaram Śāstrī has no known commentary. *Laghu Śabdenduśekhara*, as simple as Śekhara and edited in full by Rāmaśāstrī Mānavallī and Bhāradvāja Nārāyaṇaśāstrī includes a good number of commentaries. Gopala Shastri Nene (1925),

35. G. Cardona, *op.cit.*, p. 285.

36. *Op.cit.*, p. 285 'A commentary, called Prasād was written on it by the author's grandson Viṭṭhala'.

Nandkishore Śāstrī (1936). Sudāmā Miśra Śāstrī, Sadāśiva Śāstrī Jośī (1938) have contributed a lot towards the annotation and clarification of *Kaumudī* text. The *Siddhānta-Kaumudī* was also abridged by Varadarāja.[37] *Sārasiddhānta-Kaumudi* is a medium short and super short version. Bhaṭṭojī's interpretation of Pāṇini was known as *navya* (new) in contrast to earlier authors in Pāṇini.[38]

Other Commentaries

The *Kṣīrataraṅgiṇī* of Kṣīrasvāmin, the *Dhātupradīpa* of Maitreya-rakṣita and Sāyaṇa's *Mādhavīya-dhātu-vṛtti* are different versions of the *dhātupāṭha*. However all they show are the progression in discussion and the extensive work on grammar concerning the related topics whether old, new or ultra new approach to the development of grammar. It is assumed that the rules of the grammar have to account for Sanskrit usage, of whatever epoch. It is also assumed that these rules of grammar should be as concise as possible, containing no superfluous statement and fully consistent with each other. The essential aim of grammar is to arrive at an interpretation of literature which meets all requirements. Grammar is a process of learning to scrutinize and to consider a given statement or part of it truly necessary.[39] The schools of Indian

37. G. Cardona, *op.cit.*, p. 287, Vide P.K. Gode (1950).
38. N.N. Das Gupta (1936), *op.cit.*, p. 351, argued that Yavanas were Yavanas of Sogdiana and set Pāṇini's dates between 479 and 327 BC./C.V. Vaidya (1930) also pointed out that rule 2.1.70., does not show that Pāṇini postdated the Buddha. In addition, he also shows in 8.2.50 (*nirvāṇovāte*), which gives the item *nirvāṇa* (extinguished) cannot be used as evidence to show that Pāṇini was pre-Buddhism. M.S. Bhat (1959) argued to place Pāṇini after Buddha. Kātyāyana's *Pauṣkarasādī* places Pāṇini as pre-Pāṇinian teacher contemporary with Buddha.
39. Here literature is the study of Universe of Knowledge.

Philosophy envisage language as a system of communication where Pāṇini, Kātyāyana, Patañjali, *et al.* are successive teachers, to impart, to suggest and to add to the genesis of grammar (Sanskrit as well as Vedic).

3

Pāṇini's Contributions to Sanskrit Grammar

Shankar Nene

येनाक्षरसमाम्नायम् अधिगम्य मेहश्वरात्।
कृत्स्नं व्याकरणं प्रोक्तं तस्मै पाणिनये नमः॥

yenākṣarasamāmnāyam adhigamya maheśvarāt ।
kṛtsnaṁ vyākaraṇaṁ proktaṁ tasmai pāṇinaye namaḥ ॥

Introduction

VYĀKARAṆA has been described as mouth of Vedas — one of the six organs of the Vedas — and is considered to be a significant one. According to *Mahābhārata*, in Vyākaraṇa or grammar, attempts are made to expose meanings of words, to etymologically interpret them and to explain original words and suffixes, separately.[1] It is said, appropriately and correctly used and, at the same time, properly learnt one word can fulfil one's desires — temporal and spiritual. This is possible only with the knowledge of Vyākaraṇa of language.[2]

Beginning of Grammar or Vyākaraṇa

There are references in the works, more oftenly mentioned as

1. सर्वार्थानां व्याकरणाद् वैयाकरण उच्यते।
प्रत्यक्षदर्शी लोकानां सर्वदर्शी भवेन्नरः॥ प. भा., उद्योग — 36, 43)
2. "एकः शब्दः सुप्रयुक्तः सम्यग्ज्ञातः स्वर्गे लोके च कामधुक् भवति".

revelations to the sages or *ṛṣis*, according to which the first enunciator of Vyākaraṇa was Brahmā. He passed it on to Bṛhaspati, who became the first expounder or teacher and taught it to Indra. There is a very significant reference in *Mahābhāṣya* of Patañjali, according to which, Bṛhaspati began to teach Indra, word by word, without laying down any rules, applicable to the groups of words. Words are endless. One thousand years passed and still the end was nowhere in sight. Bṛhaspati got tired and the teaching was abandoned.[3]

Then it was Indra, who began to formulate some common rules to teach grammar. These rules encompassed various wider canvases, each one enveloping thousands of words in its fold. Then, groupwise charts were made and a new format of Vyākaraṇa came into being. In course of time, on an analogy of the derivation of words, an analysis of the word into its constituent elements such as the base, the affix, the augments and the modifications, was undertaken by grammarians. In fact, it was in Aindra Vyākaraṇa that groups such as *prakṛti*, *pratyaya*, etc., were formed. On the basis of this premise, it can be said that, among Vyākaraṇas, Aindra Vyākaraṇa is the oldest one.

Grammarians other than Pāṇini

After Aindra Vyākaraṇa, several grammarians composed their treatises. Pāṇini has mentioned ten of them in *Aṣṭādhyāyī*: Āpiśali, Kāśyapa, Gārgya, Gālava, Cakravarmaṇa, Bhāradvāja, Śākaṭāyana, Śākalya, Senaka and Sphoṭāyana. There were 13 grammarians who were not referred to by Pāṇini. Besides,

---

3. ब्रह्मा बृहस्पतये प्रोवाच बृहस्पतिरिन्द्राय, इन्द्रो भरद्वाजाय
भरद्वाजः ऋषिभ्यः, ऋषयो ब्राह्मणेभ्यः — (ऋक्तन्त्रम् ।, 1, 4).
बृहस्पतिरिन्द्राय दिव्यं वर्षसहस्रं प्रतिपदोक्तानां शब्दानां शब्दपारायणं प्रोवाच (व्या. म. भा., 1, 1, 1).
ते देवा इन्द्रमब्रुवन्, इमां नो वाचं व्याकुर्वंति। तामिन्द्रो मध्यतोऽवक्रम्य व्याकरोत् (तैत्तिरीयसंहिता, 6, 4, 7).

there were 42 grammarians who find mention in the Vedic Prātiśākhyas but have not been referred to by Pāṇini.[4]

After Pāṇini, several grammarians are also known to have been there. We would not discuss them as they are out of the gamut of the present discussion. Pāṇini's contribution is unique in that his innovative thoughts and linguistic techniques influenced the whole lot of subsequent grammatical traditions. Some of the salient features of Pāṇini's contributions are only briefly discussed in the following pages:

Brevity: 14 Sūtras or Aphorisms

There is a saying, making rounds among scholars, according to which a grammarian feels happy as if he has got a son, if he can do with one short vowel less. — *ekamātrālāghavena putrajanmotsavo bhavati vaiyakaraṇānām*. This saying seems absolutely justified when one reads Pāṇini's *sūtras*. His *sūtra* compositions are so compact and precise that there is no scope for omitting even one short vowel. One point here cannot be overlooked. While attempting compactness and precision nowhere in Pāṇini's *sūtras* clarity of style has been allowed to suffer. It remains intact. Nowhere stylistic unintelligibility has cropped out.

Aṣṭādhyāyī or *Aṣṭaka*, as has been named by Yudhiṣṭhira Mīmāṁsaka, is considered to be a unique thing to have happened to Sanskrit grammar and is the biggest contribution. *Aṣṭādhyāyī* contains eight chapters (*adhyāya*), again each chapter having been subdivided into four quarter-chapters (*pāda*). Number of *sūtras* are 3995 which illustrate grammatical rules, encompassing both Sanskrit and Vedic languages.

The fourteen aphorisms carry a unique and *never-before* order of letters which is very original and extremely scientific.

---

4. Harikṛṣṇaśastrī, *Sanskṛtavāṅmayam*, Kīrtisaurabha-prakāśanam, Vārāṇasī, 1989, pp. 50-54.

Pāṇini formulated his *Pratyāhāra Sūtras* on the basis of these fourteen *sūtras*. These *Pratyāhāra Sūtras* are like capsules containing squeezed unlimited meaningful substance. *Pratyāhāra* means the comprehension of several letters or affixes into one syllable, effected by combining the first letter of a *sūtra* with its final indicatory letter or, in the case of several *sūtras*, with the final letter of the last member; thus, *aṇ* is the *pratyāhāra* of *sūtra aiuṇu; ac* of the four *sūtras*: *aiuṇ, ḷṛk, aoṅ, aioc; hal* of the consonants and *al* of all letters.

There is difference of opinion in the matter, whether the whole text of *Aṣṭādhyāyī sūtras* has been authored by one person, Pāṇini, or there are interpolations. This aspect is not particularly relevant to the present discussion. Here, we can only state that the *sūtra* text of *Aṣṭādhyāyī*, in its totality, has contributed a great deal not only to the field of Sanskrit grammar, but also to the fields of the grammars of various languages, Indian and foreign.

These *sūtras* are preceded by a catalogue of sounds themselves subdivided into fourteen groups and variously called as *Pratyāhāra-Sutras* (abbreviation *Sūtras*), *Śiva-Sūtras* or *Maheśvara-Sūtras*. These *sūtras* are the ideal example of brevity of highest order. Although *sūtra* style did exist before Pāṇini, it was in Pāṇini's work that this style has reached its culmination and attained perfection in brevity. The merits of the *Śiva-Sūtras* in their grammatical aspect are very evident. For instance, the *pratyāhāra en* in the third partial *sūtra* and the *pratyāhāra aic* in the fourth *sūtra* enable the author to formulate, concisely, the rules for the *guṇa* and *vṛddhi* of *i* and *u*. Similarly, the *pratyāhāra yaṇ* contained in the 3rd and 6th *sūtra* and the *pratyāhāra ik* contained in the 2nd and 3rd *sūtra*, by their correspondence in order, facilitate the formulation of the rules bearing on the changes of semi-vowels into their correspondent vowels and vice-versa. Many other similar examples in the entire *sūtra* prove its grammatical usefulness.

Dhātupāṭha and Gaṇpāṭha

In *Aṣṭādhyāyī* are collated different grammatical rules pertaining to various groups of words in the *sūtra* format. In these rules, Pāṇini refers to groups of verbs and nominal bases in various ways. These bases appear in two ancillaries to the corpus of rules, a catalogue of roots called the *Dhātupāṭha* and a catalogue of nominal bases, called the *Gaṇapāṭha*.[5]

As mentioned above, one of the significant features of the style of Pāṇini's writing was etymological interpretation of words[6] from their verb-roots. This process is Pāṇini's invaluable gift to the field of grammar. He collated large number of verbs or *dhātus* (in this case also some scholars are not keen to ascribe authorship to Pāṇini) popularly being used by *loka* (people) and compiled them in a collection under the title *Dhātupāṭha*. Even today, this compilation serves as a very significant source and basis for the comparative studies of Āryan languages and dialects. The issue of authorship may well be disputed but there is no shred of doubt that it was Pāṇini who showed the way of making full utilization of *Dhātupāṭha*. This is his contribution.

Pāṇini's Paribhāṣās or Metarules

Paribhāṣās are auxiliary hypotheses which seek to improve or explain the procedure of Pāṇini's grammar. *Paribhāṣās* can be translated as metarules or metalanguage, principles, theorems, or auxiliary hypotheses.[7] In general, these technical words are used by linguists. For commoners these can be expressed by

---

5. Harikṛṣṇaśastrī, *Sanskṛtavāṅmayam*, Kīrtisaurabha-prakāśanam, Vārāṇasī, 1989, pp. 50-54.

6. Sūryakānta, *Sanskṛt Vāṅmaya kā Vivecanātmaka Itihāsa*, Orient Longman, New Delhi, 1972, p. 31.

7. Dominik Wujastyk, *Metarules of Pāṇinian Grammar*, Ebert Forsten Gronigen, London, U.K., 1993.

the term *paribhāṣā*s or *saṁjñā*s. Pāṇini provides a large number of rules which help in the correct utterances of the language. These rules are used to assign a structural analysis to a sentence which already exists. If we wish to express "I shall go," Pāṇini's grammar leads us through a series of selections to the forms *gamiṣyāmi* or *gantāsmi*.[8]

Pāṇini has coined his own interpretative canons and still appears to have liberally borrowed from his predecessors' words and particles. This adoption from earlier *ācārya*s adds to the glory of his work as the most complete text of Sanskrit grammar. Some earlier terms as : *auṇ* (nominative and accusative dual ending), *āṇ* (instrumental singular case-ending), *vyakti*, *vacana*, etc., can be seen interspersed with his own terminology in the corresponding rules. In his system many indicatory letters do appear in terms of prefixes, suffixes, augments and substitutes. It is important that he has offered a comprehensive explanation of such letters, which constitute some of his *paribhāṣā*s.[9]

Pāṇini laid down about 4000 brief rules of varied nature: definition (*saṁjñā*), interpretative canon (*paribhāṣa*), injunction (*vṛddhi*), restriction (*niyama*), extention (*atideśa*), governance (*adhikāra*), prohibition (*niṣedha*), repetition (*anuvāda*), option (*vibhāṣā*) and irregularity (*nipātana*). These technical expressions, in due course of time, got enriched with the necessary modifications, additions and proliferations, and eventually this process culminated into a very prolific metalanguage.[9] For the want of space, it is not possible to enumerate all such technical expressions and rules. However, some of the significant rules are as follows: *tasminniti nirdiṣṭe pūrvasya, tasmādityuttarasya,*

8. Dominik Wujastyk, *Metarules of Pāṇinian Grammar*, Ebert Forsten Gronigen, London, U.K., 1993.
9. Dās Karunasindhu, *Paribhāṣās in the Pāṇinian System of Grammar*, Sanskrit Book Depot, Calcutta, 1986, p. 24.

sthānivadbhāva, iko guṇavṛddhī, acaśca, uraṇ raparaḥ, anantyavikāre'ntyasya deśasya, ṣaṣṭhī sthāne yogā, svaṁ rūpam śabdasyāśabdasaṁjñā, arthagrahaṇe nīnarthakasya, pratipadokta, lākṣaṇika, prātipadikagrahaṇe liṅgaviśiṣṭasyāpi grahaṇam, alontyasya.

As a model, we will briefly mention only one such metarule or *paribhāṣā*, viz., *sthānivadbhāva*. As a major phenomenon in Sanskrist, every replacement involved either a letter or a word, or a certain part of it. It is not easy to determine the exact extent of what is being replaced with a substitute. For example, since a reference to a stem or so is generally inclusive of its augmented varient, it is expected that, like the unaugmented stem, which is earmarked with the sixth case-ending in a rule as the *sthānin* (original) of the intended substitute, its augmented varient too would undergo replace-ment. Moreover, the *sthānin* may, otherwise, be enlarged with a prefix or so in a compound (e.g., *nirjara*, a compound of *nir-* and *jara*).[10]

There are many other technical terms which indicate great intellectual prowess of the grammarians belonging to Pāṇinian school. Some of them are as follows:

ANUVṚTTI

We have discussed, earlier, that, instead of repeating all the letters contained in that, particularly, *sūtra* or *sūtra*s what Pāṇini does is to mention only *pratyāhāra*. Secondly, what he does is *anuvṛtti*, meaning he repeats or supplies in the following *sūtra* the same rule, which was mentioned in the preceding *sūtra*, — influence of a preceding rule on the following one. Sometimes, this act of *anuvṛtti* takes place according to the rule of *maṇḍūkapluti* or "leaps of frog." It denotes skipping over or omitting several *sūtra*s and supplying from a previous *sūtra*.

10. Dās Karunasindhu, *Paribhāṣās in the Pāṇinian System of Grammar*, Sanskrit Book Depot, Calcutta, 1986, p. 24.

KṚDANTA

Kṛdanta denotes a word ending with a *kṛt*. As mentioned above, there is a process of formulation of nouns by adding affixes or suffixes to roots to form verbal derivatives — *kṛdanta*. Pāṇini has compiled (some scholars are reluctant to ascribe authorship to Pāṇini) a long list of such *pratyaya*s or suffixes along with the corresponding connotations; formulating another noun from a noun by adding affix or suffix to denote special meaning — cf. *kṛdtiṅ* । *dhātoḥ* (3.1.91) *ityadhikāra tiṅvarjitaḥ pratyayaḥ kṛt syāt* ॥

TADDHITA

This is a term ancient grammarians, belonging to Pāṇinian school, used as *sarvanāman* or *avyaya* without giving any specific definition of it. It is worth mentioning that word *taddhita* has been used by the ancient grammarians in the sense of a word derived from a *prātipādika* by the application of suffixes like *a*, *yat*, etc., and not in the sense of words derived from roots by affixes such as *an*, *ti*, etc., which were termed *nāmakaraṇa*. Pāṇini has used the word *taddhita* not for words but for the suffixes which are added to form such words at all places. In fact, he has begun the enumeration of *taddhita* affixes by putting the term *taddhita* for affixes such as *ti*, *śaṅ*, *an*, etc.[11]

UṆĀDI SUFFIXES

There is a long-drawn controversy between the followers of Śākaṭāyana and Gārgya with regard to the derivation of words. The dispute is whether words can be broken into parts. This can be traced to the Vedic texts where derivation of the word *rudra* from √*rud*, *chandas* from √*chadi* and *deva* from √*divā* was suggested. Many more examples can be cited. According to Sthaulāṣṭhīvi *nañ>knopi-* is the stem for *agni* and in Yāska's opinion *agra*, *agra-nayana* and *agraṇī* are probable sources of

11. P. IV.1 76.

the component parts of the word. To the *Nirukta*, each and every *nāma* is derived from a verbal root. A brief account of the contrasting views of the two opposite camps, headed by the two great linguists, Śākaṭāyana and Gārgya, finds mention in *Nirukta* (1.4).

Here Pāṇini shows his synthetical skill and admits that many a word cannot be dissected into base and suffix but still accommodates *uṇādi* suffixes, which analyse words, at large. He gave his nod to *uṇādi*-suffixes and included them in his science, but did not deliberately deal with them at length and systematically. While giving his approval he kept some reservation by adding *bahulam* word after *uṇādayaḥ*.[12] By adding *bahulam* he gave full freedom to *ācārya*s to manoeuvre as much as they wished.

Svarita and Adhikāra

Pāṇini marks a particular word as *svarita*[13] and promulgates *adhikāra* — a governing rule which exerts a directing or governing influence over other rules. Putting the likes of features, as mentioned above in use, Pāṇini saves himself from the rigmarole of repetition and instils precision as an integral part of all his grammatical exercises.

Pāṇini: Aid to Vedic Exegesis

Aṣṭādhyāyī is one of the special features which also happens to be that, besides serving as a useful aid in etymologically explaining and interpreting words used in Sanskrit language, it can also serve the purpose of effecting exegeses of Vedic words. There are problems, indeed, which have been dealt with in greater details by Prof. G.V. Devasthali in his two

12. P. IV.1 76.

13. समाहारः स्वरितः — the third or a mixed tone lying between high and low.

articles: (1) "Pāṇini as an Aid to the Ṛgvedic interpretation" and (2) "Sāyaṇa utilising Pāṇini in his Ṛgvedic Bhāṣya."[14] The task of dealing with them is out of the purview of the present discussion. We can proceed further, taking for granted, that, in spite of these problems, *Aṣṭādhyāyī* is competant enough to undertake executing task of exegeses of words in Vedic literature, particularly, in the *Ṛgveda*.

Accentuation

Pāṇini has very intelligently used *anubandhas*. *Anubandha* is an indicatory syllable or letter intended to denote some peculiarity in the inflection, accent, etc., of the word, to which it is attached, as the *lṛ* in *gamlṛ* and *ṇ* in *iṇ*. One keeps wondering, why Pāṇini used some mute letters or *anubandha*s at all. Letters such as *k, c, n, t, n, p, r* and, or the face, seem quite redundant. One is enlightened on their relevance only when one gets perused with the intricacies of *svara prakriyā*. From this, one comes to know that they are extremely useful in Vedic words and very much relevant. Otherwise, these letters serve no other purpose than indicating accentuations, which have hardly any place in Sanskrit. Let us take mute *l*. If a word formed by appending a *lit* suffix, it carries an *udātta* syllable, preceding the suffix, irrespective of the base, e.g., *imàthā*. (*idam* + *thāl*), *jyeṣṭhàtāti* (*jyeṣṭha* + *tātil*), *abhítaḥ* (*abhi* + *tasil*), "Mute *r* indicates that a formation in *rit* suffix has an accent on the penultimate syllable: *upottamam riti* (6.1.217); *ripratyayāntasyopottamam udāttaṁ syāt/yadāvahnīye*".[15]

---

14. The first article was published in *Prof. H.D. Velanakar Commemoration Volume*, 1965, pp. 20-26 and second in *A Study of Sāyaṇa's Commentary on ṚV*, 1. 1-19, J.A.S. Bombay (New Series), Vol. 38, 1938, pp. 165-73.

15. G.V. Devasthali, *Pāṇini and Ṛgvedic Exegesis* in *Dr. V. Raghavan Felicitation Volume*, Eds., R.N. Dandekar, R.K. Sharma, Mandan Mishra, Satyavrata, S.S. Janaki, p. 98.

Mute *c* indicates that the formation in a *cit* suffix is oxitone or *udātta* (*anta udāttaḥ yāt*— SK.), e.g. *mahimàn* (*mahàt* + *imanic*), *tredhā* (*trī* + *edhāc*). In these examples the corresponding rules of accentuation are best illustrated. Another good example of accentuation is *kyac* formations or denominatives which invariably take the accute on *ya*, e.g., *vṛṣāyàte*, *pṛtanyàsi* (*pṛtanyà* is denominative of *pṛtanā*).[16]

Pāṇini has also laid down rules for accentuation in declension. All case endings are enclite or *anudātta*. *anudāttau suppitau* — PA.1.4; also *pūrvasyāparādaḥ*) — SK. Generally, words (particularly, ending in *a* and *ā* and other vowels) retain the accute of the base throughout. Thus, from *deve* we have *devāḥ*, *devāya*, *devebhiḥ*, *deveṣu*, from *āśā* we have *āśābhyaḥ*, *āśāḥ*.[17]

The optional monosyllabic forms of *asmad* and *yuṣmad* as also the oblique forms of *idam* when used as *anvādeśa* are enclitic. Similarly, vocatives with which a *pada* or a sentence does not begin are enclitic. But when they are at the beginning of a *pada* or a sentence, they are invariably barytone (*svarit*).

So far as accentuation in conjugation is concerned, after *akāranta* (ending in) *aṅga*, the *sārvadhātuka* personal endings are enclitic,[18] meaning, thereby, the acute of the *aṅga* is retained.

The nominative plural ending, when appended to masculine or feminine words ending in *a* or *ā* takes an augment (*asuka*) (= as). The augmented ending thus becomes *as* + *as* = *asas*: *ājjaserasuka* — PA, 7.1.50; *avarṇāntād aṅgāt parasya jaso'suk syat*: *devāsaḥ*, *brāhmaṇāsaḥ* — SK.[19]

The above rule also holds good for the vocative plural

16. G.V. Devasthali, *Pāṇini and Ṛgvedic Exegesis* in *Dr. V. Raghavan Felicitation Volume*, Eds., R.N. Dandekar, R.K. Sharma, Mandan Mishra, Satyavrata, S.S. Janaki, p. 98.

17. *Ibid.*

18. *Ibid.*

19. *Ibid.*

ending. The nominative, accusative and vocative plural ending appended to neutral words ending in *a* are often elided (*lupta*), e.g., *vànā* for *vanāni*, *yuga* for *yugāni*, *bhadra* for *bhadrāṇi*.[20] The genitive plural ending *¢m* takes the *¢gama nut* (=*n*) when appended to the word *go*, only when the word comes at the end of a *pāda* — *ut vrajam aparvatāsu gonām* but *gavam apavrajam vṛdhi*.[21]

In addition, *supāṁ sulukapūrva-savarṇāccheyāḍāḍyāyājālaḥ* (PA, 7.1.39) is very comprehensive and indicates declensional peculiarities of the Veda.[22]

In the same manner characteristics of conjugational peculiarities, verbal formations in the Vedic text can be elaborated in the light of Pāṇini's *Aṣṭādhyāyī*. Pāṇini has mentioned 15 suffixes to convey the sense of infinitive (*tum*). It is worth nothing that in case of the *anubandhas* not being brought into the use these suffixes will diminish to about 6 or 7.[23]

Vis-a-vis sandhis in the Veda, the final *ā* is nasalized — *abhra ā apaḥ*; sometimes final *an* is nasalized only if that is not *pragṛhya* — *aṇo'pragṛhyasyānunāsikaḥ* (PA 8.4.57), e.g., *nyuptāśca bahravo vācam akrata* (ṚV, 10.34.5c). The *visarga* of *saḥ* is elided before a vowel if the ellision serves to give the line the required number of syllables and thus the *pāda* is complete *so'ci lope cet pādapūraṇam* (— PA, 6.1.134).[24]

---

20. G.V. Devasthali, *Pāṇini and Ṛgvedic Exegesis* in *Dr. V. Raghavan Felicitation Volume*, Eds., R.N. Dandekar, R.K. Sharma, Mandan Mishra, Satyavrata, S.S. Janaki, p. 98.
21. *Ṛ*V. 4.20.8 and ṚV, 1.10.7.
22. *Ibid*.
23. *Ibid*.
24. Venkatasubramonia S. Iyer, *On Varients in the Aṣṭādhyāyī* in the Proceedings of the International Seminar on Pāṇini, Pune Vidyapeeth, 1982, p. 141.

To sum up, this is quite possible to learn and understand intricacies of the Vedic grammar and accentuation by applying rules laid down by Pāṇini.

Pāṇini's Use of Semantics

Pāṇini's *Aṣṭādhyāyī* illustrates semantic characteristics: (1) the preliminary feature is to derive the corresponding phonological forms by the series of replacement rules; (2) grouping words and stems into classes; (3) conveying the shades of meaning by the whole derived word or compound word. Then the shades are taken into consideration by Pāṇini as one of the conditions to assign the particular affix or compounding process.[25]

Pāṇini also made use of semantic components to distinguish members of groups semantically related when this required for the accurate description of the data, e.g., *domestic animals that are not young. A thing that is not concrete.*[26]

For ancient grammarians meaning is primary and the sound produced depends upon the meaning. Pāṇini, however, serves to connect the semantic level with the phonetic level starting from the former.

This has to be kept in mind that Pāṇini's goal was to provide, adequately, a well-described grammar for Sanskrit. His aim was not to analyse the language semantically and, as such, was not guided by semantic consideration. He used them

25. Examples of these three characteristics could be: 1. *Vartamāna*-"present time," *Bahuta* — "Plurality"; 2. *Varṇa* — "colour words", (a list is available); and 3. "Name of person" *versus* "a generic noun", "a word implying censure" *versus* "one with no such implication" — quoted in Venkatasubramonia S. Iyer , *Pāṇini's Use of Semantics* in the Proceedings of the International Seminar on Pāṇini, Pune Vidyapeeth, 1982, p. 128.

26. *Ibid.*

in *Aṣṭādhyāyī* intelligently wihtout allowing them to go against the earliar consideration. He concentrated in deriving grammatically correct phrases and sentences, but he did not show much concern to eliminate the construction of semantically relevant sentences. For him the construction of sentence such as *agnina siñcati puṣpāṇi devadattaḥ*, although semantically illogical, is a sentence grammatically correct.[27]

Pāṇini's Attitude of Synthesis

In spite of Pāṇini's firm ideas, he was not a person of unyielding or stubborn tendencies. In disputable matters, where there was a clear division of opinions among *ācārya*s, he chose the way of synthesis. He realized that some words are made by adding suffixes to the roots, or verbs, and this process is included in general or specific rules. But there is a vast treasure of words being used by common people and in case of many of these words root-suffix rule does not hold good. Such words get coined on their own and become popular among people. Pāṇini has named such words as *saṁjñā pramāṇa*.[28]

There are also some words which are not covered under any grammatical rules. Pāṇini cleverly accepts the reality and gives his sanction to such words and puts them under the category of *pṛṣodarādīni*. He accepts them to be correct and usable.[29]

Then, there is this disputable issue of the meaning of word or *śabda*. There is a long discussion on this in *Mahābhāṣya*. Ācārya Vājapyāyana believed that the word *gauḥ* denotes the whole *jāti* or species of cows — *ākṛtyabhidhānādvaikaṁ vibhaktau*

27. George Cardona, *Pāṇini: A Survey of Research*, MLBD, Delhi, 1980, p. 158.
28. *Aṣṭādhyāyī* (1.2.53), quoted in वासुदेव शरण अग्रवाल, *पाणिनिकालीन भारतवर्ष*, भूमिका, मोतीलाल बनारसीदास, दिल्ली, वि.सं. 2012, पृष्ठ 34.
29. *Aṣṭādhyāyī* (6.3.109), quoted in वासुदेव शरण अग्रवाल, *पाणिनिकालीन भारतवर्ष*, भूमिका, मोतीलाल बनारसीदास, दिल्ली, वि.सं. 2012, पृष्ठ 34.

vājpyāyanaḥ,[30] whereas according to Ācārya Vyāḍi the word *gauḥ*: denotes only one individual cow — *dravyābhidhānaṁ vaḍiḥ*.[31]

Pāṇini had already realized, there is element of truth in both these lines of arguments. In two different *sūtras* he had already stated *jātyākhyāyām ekasmin bahuvacanam anyatarasyām*.[32] He accepted that a word denotes race or species, a *jāti*, whereas in *sarūpāṇām ekaśeṣa ekavibhaktau*[33] he gives his approval to the thinking that a word or *śabda* denotes an individual *dravya*. Patañjali has briefly explained and justified Pāṇini's thinking on this matter in Paśpaśāhnika of *Mahābhāṣya*. Pāṇini, mainly with his approach of synthesis, with his concentrated mind, sharp intellect, diligence, competence in composing *sūtras* and with the help of abundance of material in terms of knowledge and information, authored science of grammar which actually presented a solution of the problems being faced by contemporary Sanskrit language. Patañjali has very rightly observed "Science of Pāṇini is great and well-composed."[34]

Patañjali's *Mahābhāṣya* is the biggest event in the history of *Pāṇiniśāstra*. Patañjali thoughtfully reflected on the Pāṇini's and Kātyāyana's works and made his imprint through *Mahābhāṣya* on the *Vyākaraṇaśāstra*. He himself was a great sort of monarch in the field of Vyākaraṇa. But with modesty, honesty and integrity of the heighest order, he also accepted Pāṇini's authority and added authenticity to his credibility. He adorned Pāṇini with the attribute of *Bhagavān*. He said: *bhagavataḥ pāṇineḥ ācāryasya siddham*.[35]

30. म. भा. 1.2.35.64.
31. म. भा. 1.2.45.64.
32. *Aṣṭādhyāyī* (1.2.58).
33. *Aṣṭādhyāyī* (1.2.64).
34. पाणिनीयं महत्सुविहितम् — (म. भा. 3. 2.3).
35. म. भा. (1.3.1).

Pāṇini's significance vis-a-vis West

A study of Indian logic in relation to Pāṇinian grammar alongside Aristotelian and Western logic in relation to Greek grammar and its successors could bring illuminating insight. Sanskrit tradition appears to have had an impact even on modern linguistic scholarship. As soon as Sanskrit became known to the Western learned world the unravelling of comparative Indo-European grammar ensued and foundations were laid for the whole nineteenth century edifice of comparative philology and historical linguistics. Nineteenth-century scholars recognized that the native tradition of phonetics in ancient India was vastly superior to Western knowledge and this had important consequences for the growth of the science of phonetics in the West.

Encyclopaedia Britannica has acknowdedged Pāṇini's significance in these words:

> "In the *Pāṇini Sūtra*s one comes across a remarkable and subtle and penitrating account of Sanskṛt Grammar. The construction of sentences, compound nouns, and the like, is explained through ordered rules operating on underlined structures in a manner strikingly similar, in part, to modes of contemporary theory. As might be imagined, this perceptive Indian grammatical work (*Aṣṭādhyāyī*) has held great fascination for twentieth century theoretical linguists."[36]

Western scholars were immensely impressed by Pāṇini's work when they came to know of it. Weber considers *Aṣṭādhyāyī* the supreme work on Vyākaraṇa, the world over, because he thinks that roots and word-forms have been extremely subtly and deeply analysed by Pāṇini. According to Goldstücker,

---

36. *Encyclopaedia Britannica*, Vol. 23, p. 50, under the head "History of Linguistics".

Pāṇini's work represents a natural development of the Sanskrit language. Even though the study of Sanskrit grammar may originally have had the practical aim of keeping the sacred Vedic texts and their commentaries pure and intact, the study of grammar in India in the first millennium BC had already become an intellectual end in itself.[37]

The development of phonetics in the West was also strongly influenced at this period as were many of the details of the more philological analysis of the Indo-European languages. By the discovery of the works of the Indian grammarians, who, from the time of the Sanskrit Grammarian Pāṇini (fifth or sixth century BC, if not before) had arrived at a much more comprehensive and scientific theory of phonetics, phonology and morphology than anything achieved in the West until the modern period.[38]

The study of the language and the corresponding writing was highly developed among the Chinese and the Indic peoples, as best exemplified by the great Indic grammarian Pāṇini and his school.[39] According to Patañjali, to speak faultlessly the Sanskrit language, one should immitate *śiṣṭas*, i.e., the learned or educated, the inhabitants of Āryāvartta. Kātyāyana had noted that Pāṇini gave lists of verbs/roots in order that certain middle Indo-Āryan forms are not to be accepted as having been correctly derived from Sanskrit verb or root. Moreover, Patañjali noted that one should study grammar in order not to use incorrect words. He has given example of such words: *helayaḥ* instead of *herayaḥ* a phrase used in calling to people, or *gavi* instead of *gauḥ*, cow. *Gavi* is a middle Indo-Āryan word. The observations of these

37. *Encyclopaedia Britannica*, Vol. 23, p. 50, under the head "History of Linguistics".

38. *Encyclopaedia Britannica*, Vol. 21, p. 52.

39. *Ibid.*, Vol. 23, p. 79.

grammarians are considered to lend support to the view that, by the sixth or fifth century BC., Sanskrit, as a medium of learned conversation coexisted with middle Indo-Āryan.[40]

40. *Encyclopaedia Britannica*, Vol. 22, p. 620.

4

Technical Devices in Aṣṭādhyāyī

P. Narayanan Namboodiri

PĀṆINI's *Aṣṭādhyāyī* has been the object of admiration for modern students of grammar due to the systematic arrangement of aphorisms regarding the rules, hither to listed, on Sanskrit words. He has expressed his regard to his ancestors by illustrating the forms derived by them in their time. More than ten grammarians are remembered in *Aṣṭādhyāyī* as a way of incorporating the regulations introduced by them. Pāṇini has also made use of the technical terms listed by the authors of Prātiśākhya and *Nirukta*. *Saṁgraha* is another text from Pāṇini, in which he framed his philosophy on language. For the considerations of Pāṇini towards language, one has to accept his broad outlook up to a certain extent. In *Aṣṭādhyāyī*, there are several apho-risms which are framed with these words *anytarasyam*, *vibhāṣa*, and *va*. Besides he has left several *gaṇas* open-ended for the sake of validity as per common usages. These two devices, introduced by him, clearly emphasize his approach toward the changing nature of language. It is interesting to note that he himself has violated his rules while applying them in certain cases — *sanādyantāḥ dhātavaḥ*, *iko yaṇaci alpāctaram liṅ cordhavamauhurtike*.

In *Pātālavijaya* a *kāvya* otherwise known as *Jāmbavatijaya* which is also attributed to Pāṇini we come across some irregular usages.

gaterddh rātre parimanda mandam
garjanti yat prāvṛṣi kālameghāḥ ।

apaśyati vatsamivendu bimbam
taccharvari gauriva huṁkaroti ॥

and
sandhyāvadhum gṛhya karena bhānuḥ

Thus, he was not much eager to establish the correctness of words with a rigid view. The work *Aṣṭādhyāyī* is thus respected and accepted by the scholars of Sanskrit grammar only because of the universally accepted concepts revealed by him with the help of his ancestors in a highly systematic way.

The date of Pāṇini has been accepted between fifth and sixth century BC. Sālanki, Sālāturīya, Dākṣiputra and Āhika are the names attributed to him. Historians have succeeded to identity the place Sālātura as Lahore which is now situated in Pakistan. One Kautsa is remembered as a student of Pāṇini both by the authors of *Mahābhaṣya* and *Kāśikā, anūṣivān kautsaḥ pāṇinim, upaśuśrūṣivān kautsaḥ Pāṇinim* — P. 3.2.108: has viewed this. The name of *upavarṣa* is considered as his teacher while the author of *Chandaś-śāstra,* Piṅgalā is his brother. The death of Pāṇini and his brother is recorded as follows.

siṁho vyākaraṇasya karturaharat prāṇān priyān pāṇineḥ
mīmāṁsākṛtamunmamādha sahasā hasti munim jaiminim ।

chandojñainānānidhim jaghāna makaro velatate piṅgalam
jñānāvṛtacetasāmatirusām korthaḥ tiraścam guṇaiḥ ॥

The organizational structure of *Aṣṭadhyāyī* can be understood only with the help of some related texts. They are the *Śiva-Śūtras, Dhātupāṭha, Gaṇapāṭha, Uṇādipātha, Phiṭsūtra* and the *Liṅgānuśāsana.*

Aṣṭādhyāyī begins with a set of fourteen *sūtras* which are either called *Maheśvara-Sūtras* or *Śiva-Sūtras*. Sound segments of Sanskrit language in the most suitable order are introduced for forming the abbreviatory terms which are the most complicated techniques. Regarding the authorship of these *sūtras* scholars carry different views. Attempts have been made by Nandikeśvara, Rājaśekhara and their followers to attribute the authority of Lord Śiva for a divine origin. While some others like Yudhiṣṭhira Mīmāṁsaka have established their authorship to Pāṇini by quoting several versions from *Mahābhāṣya*. Anyhow, it is better to follow the view put forward by Bhartṛhari in his *Mahābhāṣya-dīpikā — evamasyakṣara-samāmnāyasya na kaścidadhunikaḥ karta asti evameva vedapāram paryena smaryamanaḥ iti.*

The purpose conveyed by these *sūtras* is the forming of abbreviatory forms — *pratyāhāras*. The forms begin with the first one with an *it* would be the indicator of both the first and the intervening elements. By using the *Śiva-Sūtras*, Pāṇini has used only fortyone *prātyāhāras*. While going through the *Śiva-Sūtras* one can suspect the use of *ṇ* and *h* in two places. Problems related to the order and selection of sound segments and "*its*" are some interesting topics of investigation.

The Dhātupāṭha

Pāṇini has introduced ten groups of *dhātu* along with their augments *vikaraṇas*. By ascertaining the set of augments one is forced to believe the existence of such group of roots like *bhavādi* — 1035; *adādi* — 72; *juhotyādi* — 24; *divādi* — 140; *svādi* — 35; *tudādi* — 157; *rudhādi* — 25; *tanādi* — 10; *kriyādi* — 67; *curādi* — 441; Total 1970 *dhātus*.

Regarding the text of *Dhātupāṭha* and its authorship some controversies are there yet to be settled. Cardona has produced evidences from *Mahābhāṣya* to think of a non-Pāṇinīya list of *dhātus*, according to the view raised by Kātyāyana. On the other, Nāgeśa, the commentator of *Mahābhāṣya*, suggests that the meaning entries along with the roots are made by Bhīmasena. Palsule has also discussed this matter in detail and concluded that the meaning entries are non-Pāṇiniyan. The reference of *dhātus* in *Aṣṭādhyāyī* along with their *its* for either *ātmanepada* or *parasmaipada* termination; leads one to conlude the view that there was a listing system much earlier to Pāṇini. He successfully used the techniques of "*its*" to recognize the class of roots and their variations in meaning by *ātmanepada* and *parasmaipada* termination. The later grammanians have not given much importance to the meaning part of *dhātu* and have established the theory of multimeaningness of roots.

dhātūnām anekārthatvāt

Gaṇapātha

Gaṇapātha is an arranged listing of nominal stems. These *gaṇas* are again divided into two types. Some have a definite number while the other has no such restriction. The authorship of this portion is not free from dispute. Jinendrabuddhi, the author of *Nyāsa,* strongly opposes the authorship of Pāṇini to this *Gaṇapāṭha*. Cardona, on the other hand, suggests the authorship to Pāṇini up to a certain extent and then investigates the contribution of post-Pāṇinians in a wide-sphere. Pāṇini's usage of this *Gaṇapāṭha* should be considered as a technical device in order to bring brevity as well as clarity while explaining the nominal stems. The open-ended *gaṇas* allow to accept the correctness and validity even though they are not listed in grammar. So, it can be counted as one of the outstanding visions of Pāṇini on language.

The Uṇādi Sūtras

These *sūtras* introduce affixes to derive nominal stems. Two sections such as *pañcapadī* and *daśapadī* are found. This section helps much to attain *prātipadikatva* and *prayogārhatva* of words which are not, otherwise, derived. Śākaṭāyana, Kātyāyana and Pāṇini are the suspected authors of this text.

Pāṇini has introduced two aphorisms in connection with *uṇādi*. Such as *uṇādayo bahulam* P. 3.3.1 and *tābhayamanytroṇā dayaḥ* (P.3.4.75). The first rule that affixes *uṇ*, etc., is introduced after verb. Thus, √*kṛ+uṇ*. the form *karu* is derived — means artisan. The second rule states that *uṇādi* affixes can also be introduced to denote *kāraka*s other than *sampradāna* and *apādāna*. These two rules in the *sūtrapāṭha* clearly fix the fact that the *sūtrapāṭha* presupposed *uṇādi*. Scholars are of the opinion that Pāṇini had a text of *uṇādi*, which he used for his *sūtrapāṭha*. That version which was known to him was modified later. In *Siddhānta-Kaumudī* Bhaṭṭojī Dīkṣita has listed 751 *sūtra*s in accordance with the commentary of Jinendra. These sets of *sūtra*s are very much helpful to substantiate the theory introduced both by Śākaṭāyana and Yāska

nāmaca dhātujamaha mirukte
uyākaraṇe sakatasya ca tokam.

Phiṭsūtra

This is a small treatise dealing with the rules of accentuation of linguistic criteria. In order to attain the derivational process smooth Pāṇini has placed the aphorisms like *ādyudāttaḥ, pratyayaḥ, paraśca, anudattaḥ suppitau.*

They are thus called because this treatise begins with *phisonta udāttaḥ,* which means *pratipādika*.

Liṅgānuśāsana

The text *Liṅgānuśāsana* consists of about two hundred aphorisms which attribute the gender of nominal stems according to their meaning and structure. They are presented under the heading Feminine, Masculine, Neuter Feminine, Neuter Masculine, Neuter and Variable. The last chapter introduces a list of nouns which can be used in anyone of the genders. Pāṇini has introduced certain aphorisms on the course of his derivation which indicate the gender with significance. *Striyam ktin,* P.3.3.18; *puṁsi saṁjñāyām ghaḥ,* P. 3.3.114 According to Patañjali the gender is not taught in linguistics since it is assumed that are to be known from usages. *Liṅgamaśiṣyam lokāsrayatvālliṅgasya. Mahābhaṣya,* 2.1.36. *Liṅgānuśāsana* has taken into account the possibility of meaning while explaining the gender, *dundubhi* a large kettledrum which used with sense of *akṣa*-dice is in feminine. *Nābhi* in the sense of kṣatrīya is also in feminine. Otherwise, these words will denote the meaning kettledrum and navel, respectively. The authorship of this treatise is also debatable. Yudhiṣṭhira Mīmāṁsaka has settled this dispute, attributing the authorship to Pāṇini himself by stating the references cited by Patañjali and Kātyāyana in their course of explanation.

The above-mentioned related texts are essential for the better understanding of Pāṇinian rules. These supplimentary texts have inspired some scholars to refute the single authorship of *Aṣṭādhyāyī.*

Aṣṭādhyāyī, which contains a set of about four thousand *sūtras*, explains the words and their derivation, in detail. The text is divided into eight chapters having four *pada*s each. For the introduction of the most sophisticated technical device named *asiddhattva,* he has further devided the text into *sapādasaptādhyāyī* and *tripadī* — seven chapters and a quarter in the first section and the remaining three *pada*s in the later.

The contents of the chapters are as follows:

Chapter I	Major definitional and interpretational rules Atideśa Sūtras Ātmanepada Parasmaipada rules Kāraka

Chapter II	Compounds Nominal inflection Number gender of compounds Replacement of roots Delision by luk
Chaper III	San Kṛt Tiṅ
Chapter IV-V	Subanta Stripratyaya Taddhita
Chapter VI-VII	Doubling rules Samprasaraṇa Saṁhitā Āgama Accents Aṅga
Chapter VIII	Doubling rules relative to a Pada Accent relative to a pada

Every topic in *Aṣṭādhyāyī* is presented with a heading rule, namely *adhikārasūtra*, in order to avoid its repetition to the following *sūtras*. The commentators of Pāṇini has classified the whole aphorisms into different categories based on their nature, scope and application. The correct application of the operational rules is possible only with the help of interpretational rules. Thus, a student of grammar has to know, on which ground the *sūtras* are classified and what result can be attained by that process.

Types of *sūtras* are as follows.

1. *Technical rules* (*saṁjñā*): Rules that assign a particular item to a grammatical criteria.

2. *Interpretive rules* (*paribhāṣā*): Rules which can regulate the proper functions of interpretation as well as application.

3. *Operational rules* (*vidhi*): Rules that assign an operation to be performed.

4. *Restriction rule* (*niyama*): Which controls the scope of a given rule.

5. *Extention rule* (*atideśa*): Which expands the scope of a given entity usually by allowing the transfer of certain properties which were, otherwise, not available.

6. *Heading rules* (*adhikāra*): Rules which introduce a domain of rules sharing a common topic.

7. *Adho rule* (*nipātana*): Rules which provide forms to be treated as derived even though derivational process are missing.

8. *Negation rules* (*pratiṣedha*): Rules which counter an otherwise positive provision of a given rule.

No grammarian can be free from the usages of language denoting particular meaning which the common people consider only as the main function of language. In order to prepare an artificial language, Pāṇini has developed one which is known as technical terms in *Aṣṭādhyāyī*. The term *saṁjñā* has twofold sense as a technical term or *sampratyaya,* a name, having etymological as well as conventional meanings. The meanings of the words uttered in Pāṇinīya are regulated by the rule *svam rūpam śabdasyāśabdasanṁjñā*. P. 1.1.68.

Pāṇini has borrowed several technical terms from his predecessors like Yāska and Śaunaka. Out of the hundred technical terms, more than twenty-five are borrowed from earlier works. The technical terms can be classified into three different groups due to their suggestive meaning. *Śabda saṁjñā, artha saṁjñā* and *dharma saṁjñā* are the three devisions. *Vṛddhi, guṇa, saṁyoga, anunāsika, pragṛhya, ti, ghu, gha, aṅga, pada, bha,* are the examples of *śabda saṁjñā*. These portions denote some specific works as their *saṁjñā*. In the second category, meaning or sense of the terms is considered important such as *vibhāsa, lopa, luk, karman, kartṛ, karaṇa apādāna, adhikaraṇa. Dharma saṁjñā,* which includes the following *udātta, anudātta* and *svarita*.

Technical terms, like *nadi bhi* and *avasāna,* need special mention because they act as *varma saṁjñā* at particular instances and also as *artha saṁjñā* on other occasions. The concept of technical term, as a device of grammar, was pre-Pāṇinian which is evident from Pāṇinīya itself. Candragomin is the first grammarian who attempted to introduce a text on grammar excluding the technical terms in order to avoid ambiguity.

Some scholars have stated the flexible nature of technical terms as one of the elements of *Aṣṭādhyāyī*. On the course of grammar, a student get confused on the operational process whether the replaced come in its place or its *pūrva* or *para*: *sthāne adesaḥ uta pūrvaḥ parova*. The *paribhāṣā sūtra*s help to determine the function of operational rules on the course of discussion. Kātyāyana has also framed some metarules. Nāgeśa has presented to text on *paribhāṣā*s which he received from *bhāṣya* and the usages of common people. When dispute arises on certain occasions there *paribhāṣā*s will help. Thus, they are defined *aniyame niyamakāriṇi paribhāṣā*. These *paribhāṣā*s which carry certain case endings regulate the positions of *pratyaya, āgama* and *ādeśa*. All the *āgama*s except *vikaraṇa*s are presented along with an ablative ending and the augments can be recognized with the endings such as *t, k, m*. So the rule related to placement is restricted by the *paribhāṣā sūtra*s *Ādyantautakita,* P.1.1.46, *mitacontyatparaḥ,* P.1.147, *ādeśa*s are ruled with genitive case endings up to a certain extent. The number of syllables in *ādeśa* regulates its position. So the operational ruling method is fully controlled by the *sūtras* named *paribhāṣā* embodied with excellent techniques. In his *Paribhāṣendu Śekhara,* Nāgeśa states three types such as *vacikāni, jñāpakasiddhāni* and *nyāya-siddhāni.*

The operational rules give for a certain operation to be performed. As operation is functioned along with *kārya* and *kāryin* it is necessary to look into the derivational mechanism of *Aṣṭādhyāyī.*

Pratyaya, āgama, ādeśa, vikāsa and *lopa* are the ways of operation in *Aṣṭādhyāyī.* Affixes related to placement are explained from third to fifth chapters from which *prakṛti* they will operate and what position they accept. For the purpose of brevity the *pratyayas* are introduced under certain *adhikāra-sūtras.*

An operation which requires both a right as well a left context is defined as addition. Two types of additions are there — *Vikaraṇas* and *āgamas.* The base for the first type is always *dhātus.* Regarding the second type the *anubandhas* used along them is for recognition.

Replacement occurs both for the placed as well as the *sthānins* in *Aṣṭādhyāyī.* It can be understood by the use of genitive case which is to be replaced.

Asterbhūḥ, bruvaḥ pañcānām āditaḥ āho bruvaḥ are some examples for the stem, while *parasmaipadam* is a rule allowing the replacement of *tiptasjhi.* Deletion can also be considered as an important item for the operational mechanism. For this purpose, Pāṇini introduced four technical terms such as *adarśanam lopaḥ, pratyayasyalukṣlulupaḥ pratyayalope pratyaya-lakṣaṇam nalumatangasya,* P.1.1.60-63. By using all these terms Pāṇini allows the deletion of affixes, while the preoccurence of the affixes are not considered if they are eluded by the terms *sluluk* and *lup.*

Negation has been traditionally accepted in two types — *paryudasa* and *prasajya*: When an action is negated by the use of *nañ*, it is termed to be *prasajya*. While the same take place on account of following factor, it is called *paryudasa*. *Anṛtam na vaktavyam*, non-truth should not be spoken. The *nañ* here only negates the action. It means *abhāva*. So it makes *niṣedha* as main and *vidhi* as secondary. This kind of distinct knowledge is essential while understanding the rules of Pāṇini.

Extension — Atideśa

The functions of an extension rule is to transfer the qualities or operations to something which they do not possess, earlier. Thus, these *sūtra*s widen the scope of operation in order to understand them. Pāṇini generally uses the term *vat* along with the *sūtras*. *Lotolanvaṭsthānivadadeso analvidhau* are the examples. If *vat* is not appeared in the *atideśa sūtra* they are called *arthādideśa*s.

Options are allowed in *Aṣṭādhyāyī* with this aphorism *naveti vibhāsa*, P.1.1.44. It has three divisions *prāpta*, *aprāpta* and *ubhayatra*. The meaning of *va vikalpa* is further expanded to the terms like *anyatarasam*. By using these *anyatarasyam*, *vibhāsa* and *va*, Pāṇini tries to include maximum words which are current in usage for their grammatical correctness. He has also utilized the names of his predecessors to get these options. Ad hoc rules (*nipātana*) with many words along with derived ones in the *sūtra*s Pāṇini illustrates are not grammatically justified. Thus, he allows their validity even though they are not derived properly. Kaiyaṭa distinguishes *vidhi* and *nipātana*, thus.

> *vidhinipātanayoscāyam bhedaḥ*
> *yatra avayavāḥ nirdisyante samudāyonumiyate sah vidhi yatra tu samudāyaḥ śrūyate avayavaḥ anumīyate tannipatanam.*

The classification of rules are made to introduce certain technical skills of Pāṇini by which the whole text is almost free from ambiguity. The whole of *Aṣṭādhyāyī* is established on the pillars of *Maheśvara-Sūtras*. Pāṇini has framed forty-one *pratyāhāras* which occur during the course of explanation by using the final ending syllables of *Śiva-Sūtras*. Bhoṭṭojī Dīkṣita has further added one *ra pratyāhāra* as an abbreviatory form of both *r* and *l*. But Nāgeśa has refuted this concept in his *Laghuśabdenduśekhara*. The number of *pratyāhāras* and their structure are illustrated by the following verse:

> *syādekoṅañanavatai sena dvau traya iha kanābhyan*
> *catvārascayamābhyām pañca camābhyām śalābhyam ṣat.*

Pāṇini has not used the term *anubandha* in his work but his commentators have frequently explained this mode of operation. All the *pratyayas, dhātus, āgamas* and *ādeśas* that are introduced in this text with certain syllables are termed to be *anubandhas*. Scholars are of the opinion that the word was taken from the rituals where the animal which may be killed is *anubandhya*.

Both vowels and consonants are used as *anubandhas*. Most of the consonants except the *mahapramas* and the *tṛtiyas* are not used as it is at the end. But *da* is used at the beginning for several affixes as well as many roots. There these *anubandhas* have served several purposes.

The following seven aphorisms are dedicated to recognize and regulate in *Aṣṭādhyāyī*.

> *upadeśe ajanunāsika it*
> *halantyam*
> *na vibhaktau tusmā*
> *adirnitudavaḥ*
> *cuṭu*
> *lasakvataddhite.*

One of the most important purposes of this is that *it* is *mukha-sukhārtha* — easy articulation of words

autastakāraḥ uccāraṇārthaḥ
ikarastūccarānārthaḥ
pakaroparyukaraḥ uccāraṇārthaḥ
sthānyadeśa ca taparakaraṇam mukhasukhārtham

Pāṇini has made use of these *anubandhas* to indicate accent. More than seven *anubandha* letters have been utilized for this purpose. *Anubandhas*, like *ṇ, ñ, k,* serve the purpose of *vṛddhi* in the base of which *pratyaya* is appended. Some *anubandhas* like *k, g, n* restrict the operation of *guṇa* as well as *vṛddhi*. A major number of *dhātus* are classified either *ātmanepada* or *parasmaipada* by using these *anubandhas*. For an eager student who suspects the existence of these *anubandhas* after their denotative operation the *paribhāṣā* will reply.

uccaritapradhvaṁsinohi anubandhaḥ
lup te hi anubandhaḥ sādhyasiddhivasāt sadvat.
— *Kātantraparibhāṣā vṛtti. Paribhāṣā 24. Bhāvamiśra.*

The concept of *asiddhatva* is one of the outstanding interpretational skills explained by Pāṇini. The aphorism *pūrvatrasiddham* P. 8.2.1. means that application of a rule belonging to the later section of *Aṣṭādhyāyī* (*tripadī*) is to be treated as invalid when any rule belonging to the former portion is to be applied. In the latter section also the application of a subsequent rule is to be considered invalid when a former is to be employed.

In the euphonic combination, *dvau+ahara,* do collect two by the rule *ecoyavāyāvaḥ,* P.6.1.78 will function to get *āv* in the place of *au*. The *vakāra* of this term replaced will be eluded by the rule *lopaḥ sākalysya,* P.8.3.19 and results as *dva ahāra* one doubts whether the rule *akaḥ savarṇe dīrghaḥ,* P. 4.1.101 will function or not. When the rule for *dīrghaḥ* belonging to the *sapāda saptādhyāyī* is insisted the elusion of the resultant *v* obtained belonging to the *tripadī* group becomes invalid. That is, the *'v'* remains there. This prevents the application of the *sūtra akaḥ savarṇa dīrghaḥ*. In order to provide certain irregular application of the rules he successfully employs this technique and withholds the correctness of words and their meanings. This rule has an important role to play towards the end of *Aṣṭādhyāyī*.

The last *sūtra* of Pāṇini *a a*, P.8.4.68 states that, which was considered to be open (*vivarta*) in all the proceeding operations is now made contracted (*saṁvṛta*). Because of this difference, no euphonic rule will act there due to lack of homogeneousness. In all the proceedings of *Aṣṭādhyāyī* we are informed of the function of only *vivarta*. The organ in articulation of the short *a* is contracted but it is considered to be open in case of all other vowels. If this *samvṛtatva* is explained at the beginning of *Aṣṭādhyāyī*, several *sūtras*, connected with *a*, might have been either modified or separated due to the absense of *sāvarṇya*. So, in the examples, like *deva ālaya*, no *sandhi* rule will take place by the absense of *sāvarṇya*. So, to avoid such confusion during the course of derivational process he kept silence and last proclaimed the letter *a* as *samūrta*. So, by the *sūtra*, *pūrvatra-siddham*, a student of *Aṣṭādhyāyī* is completely not aware about the existence of *samūrta* type of *akāra*. This rule *a a* is to be regarded as non-existent when the operation of all the proceeding rules up to 8.4.67.

The concept of *asiddhatva* has been further elaborated on other occasions also. *Asiddhavadatrabhat*, *pūrvatrasiddha na sthānivat* are some examples.

Having thus collected the materials from his predecessors, which he considered more essential for his mode of operation, giving high regard to establish the credibility of four Vedas Pāṇini framed a monument in the field of linguistics. This vision on language has attracted intellectuals and scholars like Theme, Cardona and F. Stall, who have produced valuble documents on *Aṣṭādhyāyī*.

Reference

Banarji, R.S., *Concept of asiddhatva in Pāṇini*, 1984.

Banarji, S.C., *Historical Survey of Ancient Indian Grammarians*, 1996.

Cardona, George, *Pāṇini: A Survey of Research*, 1980.

Devasthali., G.V., *Anubandhas of Pāṇini*, 1967.

Dvivedi, H.P., *Studies in Pāṇini*, 1978.

Mahābhāṣya.

Sarma, M.K., *Pāṇini, Kātyāyana and Patañjali*, 1968.

Sarma, Ramanath, *The Aṣṭādhyāyī of Pāṇini*, 1987.

Vayākaraṇa Siddhāntakaumudī, 1969.

5

Development of Sanskrit Grammar after Pāṇini

Yoshiyuki Iwasaki

Introduction

THE *Aṣṭādhyāyī* of Pāṇini is a monumental product of the human intelligence, to be appreciated as an empirical science, conditioned by consistency, exhaustiveness and economy. However, its universality should not be overstated, as is occasionally done by the primers of historical and general linguistics in the West, because a living corpus, with temporal and regional peculiarities, must underlay his descriptive grammar. It is, accordingly, marvellous that Pāṇini's grammar has been handed down from teachers to students over two millenniums to the present day. Although the fact of the uninterrupted transmission bears witness to its universal value that fascinates modern linguists. It implies neither that Sanskrit has stopped changing nor that Pāṇini's system has received no modification at all. The grammarians, after Pāṇini, must have not treated the grammatical system independent of their own corpora and their efforts to adjust the system to their respective actualities must have led more or less to modification of the system. Any grammar can restrain changes, to some extent, but unrealizable is the perfect prescriptivism.

It may be pointless for us, who are not general linguists,

to attempt to prove the universal applicability of Pāṇini's grammar. We should recognize it as an ideological tenet and try to find out the historical backgrounds that have motivated the grammarians, after Pāṇini, who have come to conceive such a creed. To clarify the historicity may all the more enable us to appreciate the universal value to Pāṇini's grammar.

In the following, we will take a brief survey of the history of the Pāṇinian school, after Pāṇini, with an attempt to offer general information of the grammarians and their works so that one would enter specific spheres of research. We will not discuss such issues as are still in controversy among scholars, like unfixed bio-data of grammarians, unestablished authorship and evaluation of their theories. Readers are expected to refer to the secondary sources, listed at the end, for further information and detailed argument.

Pre-Kātyāyana

Although we know little about the development of Sanskrit grammar between Pāṇini and Kātyāyana, there is no reason for believing that there was no grammarian who wrote a commentary on the *Aṣṭādhyāyī*. The later grammarians mention many authors and works as commentators and commentaries on the *Aṣṭādhyāyī*.

We shall touch upon philosophical arguments among the ancient grammarians recorded in the *Vārttika* and the *Mahābhāṣya*. Kātyāyana proposes in his opening *vārttika* the doctrine of "eternity of the word" (*śabdanityatva*) which reflects that of the Mīmāṁsā. In this connection, Pātañjali introduces the argument in the *Saṁgraha*, a lost work of Vyāḍi, whether the word is permanent (*nitya*) or produced (*kārya*). Kātyāyana, furthermore, mentions two authors, Vājapyāyana and Vyāḍi, who hold the views, respectively, that the word denotes "form" (*ākṛti*) and that the word denotes "individual entity" (*dravya*).

Some discussions in Yāska's *Nirukta* are worthy to be here mentioned although his posteriority to Pāṇini is still open to question. While commenting on the *Nighaṇṭu*, a Vedic glossary, Yāska is occasionally engrossed in the general problems of the language. His concern about the relation between the word and the object makes him define the noun (*nāman*) and the verb (*ākhyāta*) from the semantic point of view; the noun and the verb denote "being" (*sattva*) and "becoming" (*bhāva*), respectively, whereas Pāṇini defines them purely from the formal one: "that which ends with a case ending" (*subanta*) and "that which ends with a personal ending" (*tiṅanta*), respectively. As for "becoming" equated with "action" (*kriyā*) by the later grammarians is concerned, Yāska introduces, with approval, the view of Vārṣāyaṇi that it has six kinds, i.e., "to be born" (*jāyate*), "to exist" (*asti*), "to change" (*vipariṇamate*), "to grow" (*vardhate*), "to decay" (*apa-kṣīyate*) and "to disappear" (*vinaśyati*).

Yāska also remarks on the peculiar view held by Auḍumbarāyaṇa that there is no ground for the fourfold classification of the word into noun (*nāman*), verb (*ākhyāta*), preposition (*upasarga*) and particle (*nipāta*), as there is only the sentence (*vākya*) in the mind of a speaker. He is considered a predecessor of Bhartṛhari who maintains that the sentence, the meaning of which is the intuition (*pratibhā*) of a speaker, is the only and genuine unit of the language.

Moreover, Yāska mentions opposing opinions between two etymologists, i.e., Śākaṭāyana, to whom the tradition attributes the authorship of the *Uṇādisūtra*, and Gārgya. The former claims that all words are to be reconstructed from particular verbal roots, whereas the latter is never a fundamentalist as well as Pāṇini whose standpoint is represented in his rule, *uṇadayo bahulam*(P.3.3.1).

Kātyāyana and Patañjali

The substantial history of the Pāṇinian school after Pāṇini started from Kātyāyana and Patañjali, the oldest ones of the commentators on the *Aṣṭādhyāyī* known to us, as is apparent from that the later grammarians hold both of them together with Pāṇini in great respect to call them *trimuni* ("the three sages"). Various topics discussed by the later grammarians, whichever ideological backgrounds they differ in and whichever seeming novelties they show, can be traced back to the works of *trimuni*. The development of Sanskrit grammar is the hermeneutic evolution like other *śāstra*s in India.

THEIR POSITION TO PĀṆINI

Patañjali's *Mahābhāṣya* is not a commentary in the general sense but aims at judging the validity of Kātyāyana's *Vārttika*. Through examining inadequacies and searching possible omissions in Pāṇini's rules. Kātyāyana adds necessary amendments. In the same position, basically, Patañjali examines whether the amendments made by Kātyāyana have proper grounds and are really required. Patañjali often expresses disagreement with the additional or amending *vārttika*s and finds no necessity to touch the original rules. Despite occasional disagreements, however, both Kātyāyana and Patañjali are no doubt followers of Pāṇini. We find neither doctrinal nor emotional opposition between them as is clear from that Patañjali makes only necessary revisions to *vārttika*s in the light of Pāṇini's system. Their aim is in common to make Pāṇini's system perfect.

KĀTYĀYANA

Kātyāyana, the author of the *Vārttika*, is the first of the commentators on the *Aṣṭādhyāyī* known to us. He flourished in *ca*. 250 BC and was, on Patañjali's account, from the south India. His additions to and amendments of Pāṇini's rules were brought about because the forms current at Pāṇini's time had probably become obsolete by Kātyāyana's time and their meanings had developed into different ones.

Kātyāyana is mentioned as *vārttikakāra, vākyakāra* and *kātya* and identified with Vararūci in the tradition. The authorship of the *Vājasaneyī-Prātiśākhya,* believed to be posterior to Pāṇini, is attributed to Kātyāyana on account that it contains the rules which are identical with or variants of those of Pāṇini's. His authorship of the *Kātyāyanaśrautasūtra* is uncertain. While it is doubtful that Kātyāyana belongs to the Aindra school due to a story in the *Kathā-sarit-sāgara,* it is remarkable that he occasionally reveals his archaism in terminology against Pāṇini like *svara* for *ac* in the sense of the vowel. Contrary to Pāṇini's persistently scientific attitude, Kātyāyana proposes the philosophical doctrine, i.e., "eternity of the word" (*śabda-nityatva*) that invalidates a partial substitution (*ādeśa*) in a word.

VĀRTTIKA

Kātyāyana's *Vārttika* is available as is preserved and commented on in the *Mahābhāṣya*. It is discernible from the *Mahābhāṣya* where Patañjali usually paraphrases the *vārttika* text. Besides the *vārttika*s in the short prose, the *Mahābhāṣya* contains over 250 *śloka-vārttika*s in the various metrical forms. Some of these may have been composed by Patañjali, but the rest can be hardly attributed to Kātyāyana because it is occasionally specified by *bhāradvājīya, saunāga, kuṇaravādana, vādana, sauryabhagavat* and *kuṇi*. The authors hinted at in these specifications are probably Patañjali's predecessors.

PATAÑJALI

There is no historical record about Patañjali but only legendary ones. His date has been deduced from the proper names appearing in his *Mahābhāṣya,* i.e., the middle of the second century BC from "Puṣyamitra" (*ad* P.3.2.123), "Yavana" and

"Sāketa" (*ad* P.3.2.111) and the middle of the first century BC from "Śakyavarman" (*ad* A.2.4.10).

Although scholars, like B. Liebich, supported the identification of the author of the *Mahābhāṣya* with that of the *Yogasūtra*, it is proper to consider them different on account of their less compatible vocabularies and writing styles.

MAHĀBHĀṢYA

The *Mahābhāṣya* ("The Great Commentary") of Patañjali is divided into eight *adhyāyas*, each of which is divided into four *pādas* according to the division of the *Aṣṭādhyāyī*, and again each *pāda* is divided into several *āhnikas* ("daily schedules").

Patañjali adopts the conversational style of expression. A typical argument goes as follows. Contenders for and against a *vārttika* try to justify their own opinions. To doubts (*ākṣepa*) arising in the course of their discussions a teacher gives a conclusive solution (*samādhāna, siddhānta*). When the dispute continues, questions and answers are exchanged between *ekadeśin* ("one who knows a part of the truth") and the teacher. Then, the latter gives a final answer. At times, Patañjali merely enumerates various opinions without giving a decisive conclusion and merely expresses the necessity of further investigation.

Some scholars maintained that the transmission of the *Mahābhāṣya* text had been broken off on account of the statements in the *Vākyapadīya* 2.476 onwards (Iyer's edition) and the *Rājataraṅginī* 1.176. However, F. Kielhorn's reasoning is reliable that the text was uninterruptedly handed down to us though, more or less, with alternation, in the course time.

COMMENTARIES ON THE MAHĀBHĀṢYA

Since the arguments carried out by contenders are extremely difficult to trace in the logical consistency in spite of the simplicity of Patañjali's expression, it is indispensable to rely on the commentaries.

The oldest one of the commentaries at our hands is the *Mahābhāṣya-dīpikā* or *ṭīkā* of Bhartṛhari. It is a pity that it is extant up to the seventh *āhnika* of the first *pāda* of the first *adhyāya*. The clues to the whole length comprehension of the *Mahābhāṣya* are the *Pradīpa* of Kaiyaṭa (eleventh century AD) and the *Uddyota* of Nāgojībhaṭṭa (eighteenth century AD). Different from Kaiyaṭa who is comparatively pliable, Nāgojībhaṭṭa makes every eandeavour to exclude possible *phakkikā*s ("artful interpretative tricks") to show his conservatism to Patañjali.

Bhartṛhari

PHILOSOPHY OF LANGUAGE

Besides the scientific analysis and systematization of the language, represented by Pāṇini's grammar, there was another trend of thought in the ancient Indian tradition towards speculation on the language, in general, and its nature. We find the Word (*vāc*) adored as a deity in the *Ṛgveda* and observe mystical contemplation of the word in the *Brāhmaṇa* literature and numerous *Volksetymologien* in the Upaniṣads with the attempt to reach the nature of the object denoted by the word.

As we have already observed, Yāska mentions in his *Nirukta* the sages who absorb themselves in the philosophical interpretation of the word. So does also Kātyāyana and he himself proposes the doctrine *śabdanityatva* in his *Vārttika*. In the same way, Mīmāṁsakas, Vedāntins, Naiyāyikas and Buddhists developed the philosophical investigation of the word, the meaning and their relation, based upon their own ontological and epistemological backgrounds. Philosophy of language has, thus, occupied an important position in the history of the Indian philosophy.

Of the Pāṇinian grammarians, Bhartṛhari (mid fifth-sixth century AD) is the most important one who established the philosophy of language. Having the Vedāntic monism and the Pāṇinian grammar as his metaphysical and linguistic backgrounds, respectively, he deals with metaphysical, ontological and epistemological issues under the influence of the then various philosophical schools. For instance, Bhartṛhari is similar in some points to his contemporary Diṅnāga, a Buddhist logico-epistemologist, while Buddhists keenly refute his doctrine of *śabda-Brahman*, representing the metaphysical basis of the Pāṇinian school.

VĀKYAPADĪYA

The *Vākyapadīya* is *magnum opus* of Bhartṛhari, which contains more than two thousand verses. It comprises three books, i.e., the *Brahmakāṇḍa* or the *Āgamasamuccaya*, the *Vākyakāṇḍa* and the *Padakāṇḍa* or the *Prakīrṇaka*. Therefore, the *Vākyapadīya* is also called the T*rikāṇḍī* according to Helārāja's account.

The *Brahmakāṇḍa* is the opening and the smallest book containing, approximately, 180 verses. It mainly deals with metaphysics and various epistemological issues. According to Bhartṛhari, any worldly event is "manifestation" (*vivarta*) of the highest being, *śabda-Brahman*. Since the variety and the multiplicity of empirical phenomena are caused by humane "nescience" (*avidyā*) from the viewpoint of *śabda-Brahman* as the supreme reality, one has to study the grammar in order to attain "enlightenment" (*mokṣa*). The *Brahmakāṇḍa* also deals with the doctrine of *sphoṭa* to be the essential meaning, which has come to occupy one of the main issues in the field of the philosophy of language.

The *Vākyakāṇḍa* is the second book containing about 400 verses. Taking into account the views of the Mīmāṁsā and others, Bhartṛhari mainly discusses "sentence" (*vākya*) as the genuine unit of an expression, the meaning of which is "intuition" (*pratibhā*) of a speaker. Words, bases and suffixes as its constituents are mere "abstraction" (*apoddhāra*) for the sake of convenience.

The *Padakāṇḍa* or the *Prakīrṇaka* is the voluminous book which contains, approximately, 1300 verses. It deals with the specific issues on various linguistic theories, almost all of which originate in Pāṇini's rules or the discussions found in the *Mahābhāṣya*. The *Padakāṇḍa* is divided into fourteen chapters called "instructions" (*samuddeśa*s), each of which explores in depth "generic property" (*jāti*), "substance" (*dravya*), "connection" (*saṁbandha*) "substance (reconsidered)" (*bhūyo-dravya*), "quality" (*guṇa*), "space" (*diś*), "mean" (*sādhana*), "action" (*kriyā*), "time" (*kāla*), "person" (*puruṣa*), "number" (*saṅkhyā*), "possession of the result of an action" (*upagraha*), "gender" (*liṅga*) and "morphological integration" (*vṛtti*).

COMMENTARIES ON THE VĀKYAPADĪYA

There are four available commentaries on the *Vākyapadīya* as well as ones which were composed by modern *paṇḍits*.

The *Svopajñavṛtti* is the oldest extant commentary on the *Brahmakāṇḍa* and the *Vākyakāṇḍa*. The authorship has been traditionally attributed to Bhartṛhari. The *Paddhati* is the commentary on the *Brahmakāṇḍa* along with *Svopajñavṛtti*. Less information is at our hand about the author Vṛṣabhadeva whom scholars date at seventh century AD. The *Ṭīkā* is the commentary on the *Vākyakāṇḍa*, written by Puṇyarāja, about whom almost nothing has been clarified. Although he seems to have written a commentary on the *Brahmakāṇḍa*, according to the opening passage of the *Ṭīkā*, its existence has not been attested. The *Prakīrṇaprakāśa* is the commentary on the *Padakāṇḍa*, which is composed by Helārāja (tenth century AD). On account of its opening statement, it is assumed that Helārāja also wrote commentaries on the *Brahmakāṇḍa* and the *Vākyakāṇḍa*, neither of which has been handed down to us.

Kāśikāvṛtti

The *Kāśikāvṛtti*, the joint work of Jayāditya and Vāmana, is the oldest and the most popular one of the running commentaries on the *Aṣṭādhyāyī* because of its lucid manner in which it makes Pāṇini's rules plain by indicating *anuvṛtti*s succinctly and providing ample illustrations for each rule. Based upon the *Mahābhāṣya* mainly, the *Kāśikāvṛtti* is remarkable due to the *Cāndravyākaraṇa*, in a great degree. And divergences in views are observable between Jayāditya and Vāmana.

It has been traditionally accepted that, after the death of Jayāditya (mid seventh century AD) who commented on the first five *adhyāya*s, Vāmana successively wrote the rest. However, there are scholars who claim that once Jayāditya wrote running commentary on all the *adhyāya*s and, Pāṇini illustrates thereafter, Vāmana supplemented it. Thus, notwithstanding its popularity, actual phases of this work have not been clarified. After the critical edition, published from the Osmania University in Hyderabad, more detailed philological research has been going on, jointly, between India and the Europe. It is highly expected that its achievement would make a large contribution to the study of the *Kāśikāvṛtti*.

COMMENTARIES ON THE KĀŚIKĀVṚTTI

There are two important commentaries on the *Kāśikāvṛtti*.

The *Kāśikāvivaraṇapañjikā* alias *Nyāsa* of a Buddhist Jinendrabuddhi (*ca.* eighth century AD) is the voluminous commentary which follows closely on the lines of the *Kāśikāvṛtti*. He offers contemporary ideas and tries to incorporate them into his interpretation of the *Kāśikāvṛtti*. At times, he demonstrates redundancy of Kātyāyana's *vārttika*s.

The *Nyāsa* has two sub-commentaries, i.e., the *Anunyāsa* of Indumitra and the *Tantrapradīpa* of Maitreyarakṣita.

The *Padamañjarī* of Haradatta (thirteenth century AD) is the most exhaustive and explanatory commentary on the *Kāśikāvṛtti*. It also deserves to be treated as a compendium of the *Kāśikāvṛtti* study of his time because of many quotations of the passages and the verses from the *Mahābhāṣya*, the *Vākyapadīya*, the *Nyāsa* and the *Pradīpa*. Its great popularity is implied by the fact that the grammarians of the Benaras school followed the *Padamañjarī* composed in the south India more than the *Nyāsa*.

Commentaries on the Aṣṭādhyāyī after the Kāśikāvṛtti

The *Bhāgavṛtti* of Vimalamati (*ca* ninth century AD) is known only from its quotation in other grammatical works. The *Bhāṣāvṛtti* of a Buddhist Puruṣottamadeva (twelfth century AD) does not deal with Vedic rules as the title indicates but is comprehensive and full of illustrations. The *Durghaṭavṛtti* of Śaraṇadeva (twelfth century AD), though not covering all the rules, is unique in the style of questions and answers and an abundance of illustrations from the literary works.

Rearrangement of Pāṇini's rules

Pāṇini's system of grammar offers the theoretical exposition of the linguistic structure of Sanskrit to those who already have a high command. Therefore, it is quite natural that non-speakers of Sanskrit needed practical and instructive grammars. This tendency may have more grown as religions and thoughts originating in non-Brāhmaṇical societies were more on the rise. So it is never an accident that Dharmakīrti (*ca*. tenth century AD), a Buddhist from Sri Lanka, composed the first such work within the framework of the Pāṇinian tradition. The *Rūpāvatāra* of Dharmakīrti is said to be a brief summary which is arranged, often with paradigmatic illustrations, according to topics like the *Kātantra*. Thereafter, many other works in the style of rearrangement, so-called the *prakriyā* style, of the *Aṣṭādhyāyī* were produced, i.e., *Rūpamālā* of Vimalasarasvatī (fourteenth century AD), the *Prakriyākaumudī* of Rāmacandra (fourteenth or fifteenth century AD), the *Prakriyāsarvasva* of Nārāyaṇabhaṭṭa (seventeenth century AD), the *Siddhāntakaumudī* of Bhaṭṭojidīkṣita (seventeenth century AD) and the forth.

BHAṬṬOJĪ DĪKṢITA

Bhaṭṭojī Dīkṣita (sixteenth-seventeenth century AD), a Telugu brāhmaṇa, is the foremost in the Dīkṣita family who produced several other names in the fields of grammar and lexicography. He lived in Vārāṇasī where he built up his school and wrote several scholarly works. Of these the *Śabdakaustubha* is a voluminous commentary on the *Aṣṭādhyāyī*. It is mainly based on the *Mahābhāṣya* and left incomplete up to the fourth *adhyāya* though it is similar in plan to the *Kāśikāvṛtti* as a running commentary.

SIDDHĀNTA-KAUMUDĪ

The *Siddhānta-Kaumudī* of Bhaṭṭojī Dīkṣita occupies the most important position in the rearrangements of the *Aṣṭādhyāyī*. In fact, it has replaced all of the other previous works composed in the *prakriyā* style. All the rules are classified into the categories compatible with those of modern grammars in the West, i.e., euphonic combination, nominal inflection, verbal conjugation, primary (including the *uṇādi*) and secondary derivations and compound along with the Vedic forms, accent (*svara*) and gender (*liṅga*) as supplements.

The great popularity of the *Siddhānta-Kaumudī* is gauged by the rise of its several abridgements, i.e., the *Madhya-*, *Laghu-* and *Sāra-siddhānta-kaumudī* of Varadarāja and the auto-commentaries, i.e., *Bālamanoramā* for students and the *Prauḍhamanoramā* for scholars, to the latter of which Nāgojībhaṭṭa wrote the *Bṛhacchabdenduśekhara*.

It is to be noted that the rearrangement found in the *Siddhānta-Kaumudī* is not necessarily beneficial to easy comprehension as that of the practical grammars, produced by non-Pāṇinians. It rather requires a good knowledge of the whole system of the *Aṣṭādhyāyī*. A novice must be patient with that the original strings of *sūtras* are broken off and the contextual continuation of the words (*anuvṛtti*) is consequently shaded. Although it is true that the works in the *prakriyā* style were composed in need of practical grammars, Bhaṭṭojī Dīkṣita, as a traditional Pāṇinian, neither simplifies nor modifies Pāṇini's system itself as non-Pāṇinians do.

Kauṇḍabhaṭṭa and his works

Kauṇḍabhaṭṭa (seventeenth century AD) is a nephew of Bhaṭṭojī Dīkṣita and the author of the *Vaiyākaraṇābhūṣaṇa*. This work is the discursive gloss on the *Vaiyākaraṇamatonmajjana* of his uncle which consists of the verses extracted from *Vākyapadīya* of Bhartṛhari. Therefore, the *Vaiyākaraṇābhūṣaṇa* deserves to be such a commentary on the *Vākyapadīya* as, therein, incorporates various views and theories in the field of the philosophy of language down to his time, i.e., the nature of the sound, the relation between the word and the meaning, the sentence and its component parts, the *sphoṭa* theory and so forth. Kauṇḍabhaṭṭa defends grammarians' views against those of Naiyāyikas' and Mīmāṁsakas'. He also composed the *Vaiyākaraṇābhūṣaṇasāra*, the abridgement of the *Vaiyākaraṇābhūṣaṇa*.

Nāgojībhaṭṭa and his works

Nāgojībhaṭṭa or Nāgeśabhaṭṭa (seventeenth-eighteenth

century AD) who is a versatile writer from the Dīkṣita family has been endowed with the final authority of the Pāṇinian school. His literary activity ranges extensively over the Nyāya, the Sāṅkhya, the Yoga, and the Alaṅkāra and Dharma-śāstras. And he, himself, is under the influence of the Kāśmīr Śaiva.

Of his commentarial works in the field of Sanskrit grammar, the *Uddyota*, a commentary on Kaiyaṭa's *Pradīpa*, is an important clue to comprehension of the *Mahābhāṣya* as well as the *Pradīpa*. Nāgojībhaṭṭa also wrote the commentaries on the works of Bhaṭṭojī Dīkṣita, i.e., the *Viṣampadī* on the *Śabdakaustubha* and the *Bṛhacchabdenduśekhara* in shorter and longer versions on the *Prauḍhamanoramā*.

An independent work of Nāgojībhaṭṭa, worthy to be mentioned, is the *Vaiyākaraṇasiddhāntamañjūṣā* which has two other versions, i.e., the *Laghu-mañjūṣā*, shorter, and the *Paramalaghumañjūṣā*, shortest. These works rely upon Bhartṛhari's *Vākyapadīya* indepth as is evident from many quotations. Therefore, it is not too much to say that the *Mañjūṣās* are equivalent to selective glosses on the *Vākyapadīya* like Kauṇḍabhaṭṭa's *Vaiyākaraṇābhūṣaṇa* and *sāra*. Nāgojībhaṭṭa tries to establish grammarians' views mainly against Naiyāyikas and Mīmāṁsakas. He also composed the *Sphoṭavāda*, an independent work on the *sphoṭa* theory. It is doubtful that he recognizes in this work *Sphoṭāyana* mentioned by Pāṇini as its first advocator.

The *Paribhāṣenduśekhara* is one of his works by which he deserves to be the last authority of the Pāṇinian school. In this work, Nāgojībhaṭṭa collects metarules (*paribhāṣās*) applicable to Pāṇini's grammar. Thus, the Pāṇinian school has reached the height of theorization. He criticizes previous attempts to find out metarules other than those recognized in *Mahābhāṣya*. In other words, to Nāgojībhaṭṭa, an attempt to discover a metarule anywhere other than in the *Mahābhāṣya* is one to invent a new metarule and may consequently deteriorate Pāṇini's system of grammar.

Other Systems of Sanskrit Grammar

Sanskrit is the chief support of the Brāhmaṇism in the sense that a language represents the authority over the society where the language is spoken. With the growth of the non-traditional trends of religions and philosophies, their bearers needed to use Sanskrit to rival the establishment in verbally expressing their own religious and philosophical thoughts. Pāṇini's grammar was of less practical use to such people because of its elaborate and complicate system. It is, thus, natural that Buddhist and Jain scholars were under the necessity of obtaining their own grammars. While omitting the Vedic and accent rules, they adopt amendments and additions made by Kātyāyana and Patañjali at their own directions so that their grammars reflect the languages proper to their religions and philosophies. Thereby, they attach greater importance to the pursuit of comprehensiveness than to that of the consistency of the system. In this way, many schools of Sanskrit grammar other than the Pāṇinian school appeared and spread, some of which laid groundworks to the indigenous grammars outside India like Pāli and Tibetan grammars.

KĀTANTRA SCHOOL

The *Kātantra* is the oldest one of the non-Pāṇinian grammars at our hands. It served a model to the Pāli grammar of Kaccāyana, exerted influence on Draviḍian grammars and was transmitted to Tibet. It spread over the East Bangal, Kaśmīr and Nepal till modern times. There is no credible data about the Buddhist author, Śarvavarman, (probably after AD 300). His date was inferred by H. Lüders who took a philological survey of the fragmental manuscripts of the *Kaumāralāta* which is supposed to be archetype of the *Kātantra*.

The *Kātantra*, accompanied with the commentary of Durgasiṁha (eighth century AD), consists of four *prakaraṇas* which contain five, six, eight, and six *pādas*, respectively. As well as the *Aṣṭādhyāyī*, it has the supplemental literature, i.e., the *Dhātupāṭha* (extent in the Tibetan translation), the *Uṇādisūtra* along with Durgasiṁha's commentary, the *Paribhāṣā*, compiled by Durgasiṁha and the *Liṅgānuśāsana*, composed by Durgasiṁha, along with his own commentary.

CĀNDRA SCHOOL

Besides the *Kātantra*, the *Cāndravyākaraṇa* of Candragomin (*ca.* fifth century AD) was also popular among Buddhists. It seems to have spread over Tibet, as is guessed from the fact that the Tanjur contains its Tibetan translation along with those of its supplemental literature and commentaries.

The *Cāndravyākaraṇa* comprises six *adhyāyas*, each of which contains four *pādas*, respectively. Without using Pāṇini's technical terms, it not only covers the whole scheme of the *Aṣṭādhyāyī* except for the Vedic and accent rules but also exploits revisions and additions, made by Kātyāyana and Patañjali. Moreover, it enlarges the contents by adding new rules. The *Kāśikāvṛtti* remarkably quotes about 30 *sūtras* from *Cāndravyākaraṇa*.

Whether the authorship of the *Cāndravṛtti* can be attributed to Candragomin, it gave rise to controversy among scholars. R. Birwé attributes only the first four *adhyāyas* to Candragomin according to the contextual inconsistency with the fifth and sixth *adhyāyas*.

OTHER SCHOOLS

A Jain Devanandin *alias* Pūjyapāda (seventh century AD) is the founder of the Jainendra school. The *Jainendravyākaraṇa*, which consists of four *adhyāyas* with respective four *pādas*, is based on the *Cāndravyākaraṇa* and known to the authors of the *Kāśikāvṛtti*. It is handed down in the two versions; the shorter one accompanied with the *Mahāvṛtti* of Abhayanandin (*ca.* AD 750) contains about three thousand *sūtras* and the longer one, accompanied with the *Śabdārṇavacandrikā* of Somadeva, (thirteenth century AD) contains about 700 *sūtras* extra. It is supposed to have declined so early that its history after the thirteenth century is unknown.

The *Śākaṭāyanavyākaraṇa* or the *Śabdānuśāsana* is also much due to *Cāndravyākaraṇa* and utilized by Hemacandra. A Jain Śākaṭāyana (*ca.* ninth century AD) is called Abhinava-Śākatāyaṇa so as to distinguish him from another Śākaṭāyaṇa, an ancient grammarian, prior to Pāṇini. The *Śākaṭāyanavyākaraṇa* contains over 3200 *sūtras* in four *adhyāyas* with respective four *pādas*. The arrangement of the rules is already approximate to the *prakriyā* style like that of the *Siddhānta-Kaumudī*.

Hemacandra (twelfth century AD), a Jain multi-writer from Gujarat, composed the *Śabdānuśāsana* in eight *adhyāyas*, the last of which remarkably deals with Prākṛt grammar. It makes use of the *Śākaṭāyanavyākaraṇa* with the commentary, the *Amoghavṛtti*, and is arranged simply for the sake of practical use. Hence, Hemacandra's grammar came to occupy the important position among Jains in place of the *Śākaṭāyana-vyākaraṇa*. Its popularity of long-standing is evident from the fact that many commentaries and abridgements were written on it.

The *Sārasvatavyākaraṇa*, with extreme simplicity and brevity, is supposed to have been composed in the thirteenth century by an unknown author under the patronage of a Muslim dominator. This school is represented by a commentator Anubhūtisvarūpa and his *Sārasvataprakriyā* or *Sarasvatīprakriyā*.

The *Mugdhabodha* of Vopadeva (thirteenth century AD) is characterized by its brevity and simplicity. Many existing commentaries and sub-commentaries prove its popularity. However, it came to be used only in Bengal after seventeenth century since its extreme brevity and simple rearrangement may have inconvenienced those who had gotten used to Pāṇini's system.

Kramadīśvara (twelfth-thirteenth century AD) established the Jaumara school in the West Bengal. The *Saṁkṣiptasāra* of Kramadīśvara consists of the *sūtrapāṭha* and the *vṛtti* and deals with Prākṛt grammar. It is remarkable that many illustrations are taken from the *Bhaṭṭikāvya*.

There are many other grammars like the *Saupadma-vyākaraṇa* of Padmanābhadatta (fourteenth century AD), the *Sarasvatīkaṇṭhābharaṇa* of Bhojadeva (eleventh century AD), the *Śabdānuśāsana* (mid-twelfth century AD) of Malayagiri, the *Harināmāmṛta* (fifteenth century AD) of Rūpagosvāmin and Jīvagosvāmin and so on.

Conclusion — Survey of Current Studies

We made a hurried survey of the history of Sanskrit grammar, after Pāṇini. There is no room for sketching grammars of Pāli, other Prākṛts, Draviḍian and Tibetan on which Sanskrit grammars represented by Pāṇini's exerted enormous influence. In conclusion, we shall give a rough sketch of current studies of Sanskrit grammar in the West, especially, for young Indian readers' benefit.

After the Second World War, two erudite scholars have established their methods of research. P. Thieme (Germany) carries out thoroughly critical research on primary sources and, hence, clarifies their historicity. The late L. Renou (France) carefully investigated traditional interpretations and regarded cultural and religious backgrounds, with respect. The former method is succeeded by his disciples. A. Wezler (Germany) in his studies of the *paribhāṣās* does some detailed researches of grammar and painstakingly researches on the *Mahābhāṣya*, etc., while Th. Oberlies (Germany), does his consecutive research of the *Cāndravyākaraṇa*. As for the latter is concerned, careful investigation of traditional interpretations is realized in J. Filliozat (France)'s massive but suspended translation of the *Mahābhāṣya* along with the *Pradīpa* and the *Uddyota*. Cultural and religious backgrounds were esteemed by a romance, the late S. Al-George (Romania) who also had interest in modern linguistics.

J. Bronkhorst (Switzerland), active in the broad field of Indology, has contributed to various and specific studies of Sanskrit linguistics. For instance, on the Prātiśākhya literature, *paribhāṣā*s and on Bhartṛhari in both the *Vākyapadīya* and the *Mahābhāṣyadīpikā* and so forth. J.E.M. Houben (Netherlands), who has contributed to the study of Vedic rituals, has brought out selective and detailed studies of the *Vākyapadīya* and also translated a chapter with his exegeses in the light of the interaction with the contemporary philosophical trends.

J. Benson (UK) with profound knowledge of the Pāṇinian grammar is distinguished for his detailed study of the *Mahābhāṣya*. E. Kahrs (UK), taking up Yāska's etymology and other subjects, studies the essential thoughts underlying the Indian linguistic tradition. He has achieved great eminence in the field of Pāli grammar.

G. Cardona (USA), who has respect for the tradition in India, is distinguished for his massive and comprehensive achievements over the whole Pāṇini's grammar. P. Kiparsky (USA), also a specialist of generative phonology, stands on the top of the theoretical explication of Pāṇini's system.

M.V. Deshpande (USA) and A. Aklujkar (Canada) are from India where they were trained in the traditional manner. The former studies Sanskrit grammar with historical, theoretical and socio-linguistic interests. He has recently effected the textual criticism of the Prātiśākhya literature. The latter excels in his philologically and interpretatively well-balanced approach to Bhartṛhari.

References

Banerji, Sures Chandra, *Historical Survey of Ancient Indian Grammars (Sanskrit, Pāli and Prakṛt)*, Delhi, 1996.

Belvalkar, Shripad Krishana, *An Account of the Different Existing Systems of Sanskrit Grammar, Being Vishwanath Narayan Mandlik Gold Medal Prize-Essay for 1909*, 1915, Poona.

Cardona, George, *Pāṇini: A Survey of Research*, 1976, The Hague (rep. in Delhi, 1980).

Coward, Harold/Raja, Kunjunni K., *The Philosophy of the Grammarians*, Potter, Karl, Ed., *Encyclopedia of Indian Philosophies*, vol. V, 1990, New Delhi.

Saini, Ranjit Singh, *Post-Pāṇinian Systems of Sanskrit Grammar*, 1999, Delhi.

Scharfe, Hartmut, *Grammatical Literature*, Gonda, Jan, Ed., *A History of Indian Literature*, Vol. V, Fasc. 2, 1977, Wiesbaden.

Yudhiṣṭhira Mīmāṁsaka, *Saṁskṛta Vyākaraṇa śāstra kā Itihāsa*, 3 Vols., 1973, Sonepat.

6

Contributions of Kātyāyana to the Pāṇinian Grammar[1]

Malhar Kulkarni

Introduction

THE grammar of Pāṇini (from now on P) is considered as one of the best of its types throughout the world. It is written in the terse style which is a unique feature of its own. Naturally, they need an elucidation in the form of a commentary, for a common student to understand it. The fist name that occurs to one's mind, in this regard, naturally, is the "Vārttikas of Kātyāyana." In this chapter, an attempt is made to study the contributions of Kātyāyana (from now on K) towards understanding the grammar of P. It is also attempted to take a survey of the works done by the modern scholars since the last couple centuries, in this regard.

There are basically two approaches, the traditional approach and the modern Western approach. Both these approaches have peculiarities of their own, which present them in different perspectives. Let us study these approaches a little more in details.

---

1. I express my deep sense of gratitude towards Prof. Saroja Bhate who allowed me to write this article. I also thank the authrorities who accepted this for publication.

Traditional Approach

For the present-day tradition, K is considered as one of the three *munis*, the three pioneers of the science of grammar of Sanskrit, composed by P. The tradition defines the *vārttika* as — *uktānuktaduruktānām cintā yatra pravartate tam grantham vārttikam prāhuḥ vārttikajñāḥ manīṣiṇaḥ.*[2] This verse means the treatise which ponders over what has been already stated by P and what is not said by P and also that which is ambiguously stated by P. Thus, the aim of K in composing these *vārttika*s seems to be to comment on the *sūtra*s of P and make them abreast with the new material that came to light in the course of time.

It is also said that the word *vārttika* indicates that it was written on some *vṛtti*, probably, lost during the course of time. The tradition ascribes different names to K. They are Kātya, Punarvasu, Medhājit, Vararūci.[3]

There are in all 4293 *vārttika*s, composed by K. There are various names like *vākya, vyākhyānasūtra, bhāṣyasūtra, anutatantra* and *anusmṛti,* ascribed to the *vārttika*s. K is believed to have composed these *vārttika*s at around 250 BC. There were several *vārttikakāra*s before and after K. K refers to some of them, namely, Vājapyātyana, Vyāḍī and Pauṣkarasādi, in his *vārttika*s. The *vārttika*s are also found in the form of a *śloka*.

Modern Studies Related to K

Modern scholars for the last almost two centuries have devoted quite a lot of attention towards explaining and emphasizing

---

2. *Pārāśaraopapurāṇa*, Ed. Kapildev Tripathy, Sampurananandа Sanskrit Visvavidyalaya, Vārāṇasī, 1990, XVIII.19-20.
3. See *Saṁskṛta Vyākaraṇaśāstra kā itihāsa*, Pt. Yudhiṣṭhira Mīmāṁsaka, Ramlal Kapur Trust, Bahalgarh, Sonepat, Haryana, 1972, Vol. 1, p. 295.

the important place that K enjoys in the tradition of Pāṇinian grammar. Following is a brief survey of search carried out in these two centuries focusing mainly on the issue of the K and its importance in the field of the Sanskrit grammar.

The main issues regarding K, around which the discussion revolves are:

1. Was K an antagonist of P and Patañjali his defender.
2. Were K and Patañjali adherents of two different systems?
3. Historical change as a motivation for some of K's *vārttika*s?

Prof. Cardona[4] in his surveys has discussed these issues in main. He has reviewed various positions taken by different scholars since the nineteenth century. Let us take a look at these discussions in brief:

1. Two main lines of thought are visible from these records, namely, one school of scholars who thinks that K was the critic of P and Patañjali was the defender of P against K. Scholars like Goldstücker, Weber, Burnell and Böthlingk adhered to this view. The other school of thought believes this view to be improper and instead it says that both K and Patañjali had, as their aim, to discuss the rules and test their validity and consistency. This view was adhered to by R.G. Bhandarkar and Kielhorn. This view was supported by most of the later scholars, including Thieme and Vedapati Miśra.
2. Some scholars have opined that K belonged to a different school of grammar than did P and Patañjali

4. See G. Cardona, *Pāṇini: A Survey of Research*, Motilal Banarsidass, New Delhi, 1976, pp. 247-53.

tradition. A story recorded in the *Kathā-sarit-sāgara* is used as a main source in this regard by these scholars. It was also stated that P and Patañjali were descriptive grammarians as opposed to K whose views were more philosophical.

3. Scholars have argued that there is evidence that shows that P and K were separated by an interval of time sufficient to permit: grammatical forms current at the time of P to become obsolete by the time of K, words to develop different meanings, words and meanings to become obsolete. Some scholars state that K introduced additional statements to account for the derivation of the new forms. It was also stated that both K and Patañjali look upon the grammar of P as a code containing the laws of correct word formation and make the assumption that this code must be valid for all times. Some scholars think that the duty of K was not to justify or to defend P but to introduce the necessary modifications in order to keep P abreast of later developments in the language. According to them, the main purpose was to suppliment the grammar of P.

Contributions of K

Indeed, K has, critically, commented of the *sūtras* of P, has suggested many modifications in the existing *sūtras* and has added extensively new material that possibly came to light after P. His remarks mainly cater to the field of the derivational system, P has so effectively employed in the organization of his grammar. He also discusses meanings of several words used by P in his work. There is elaborate discussion of several *paribhāṣās* in his comments. It seems that it was he who introduced different *paribhāṣās* in the system which were later on developed by the *Mbh*. It was he who introduced the system of "Pūrvapakṣa and Uttarapakṣa" in the P's grammatical tradition. It can also be said although with less degree of certainty, that this "Pūrvapakṣa and Uttarapakṣa" style might have had some correlation with the fully developed system of *adhikaraṇa* of the Mīmaṁsakas. There are numerous cases like that where K has made his point and has contributed to the development of the system of P's grammar. Now, let us study these, one by one.

The definition of the *vārttika* is stated before. Indeed, the way K has commented can be considered as the first and the foremost contribution of immense importance of K. There is another definition given in the *Viṣṇudharmottara Purāṇa*[5], which explains the nature of the *vārttikas* in detail. It is

> *prayojanaṁ saṁśayanirṇayau ca vyākhyāviśeṣo guru-lāghavaṁ ca* ।
> *kṛtavyudāso'kṛtaśāsanaṁ ca sa vārttiko dharmaguṇoṣṭakaś ca* ॥

According to this definition, there are eight features of the *vārttikas*[6] namely,

1. *Prayojana* — Which refers to the purpose or the necessity of the word in the particular *sūtra* for example, *vārttika* 1 on 1.1.3 namely *iggrahaṇam ātsaṁdhyakṣaravyañjananivṛttyartham*, which states the purpose and the necessity of the word *ik* in the *sūtra*.

2. *Saṁśaya* — This refers to the raising of the doubt about a particular word of the *sūtra*, for example, *vārttika* 1 on 6.3.66, namely, *khiti hrasvāprasiddhir anajantatvāt*

5. 3.6.1.

6. For a detailed exposition of all these aspects, see Madhusudan Mishra, *Critical studies of the Vārttikas of Kātyāyana* (a dissertation, submitted to the University of Pune for the degree of Ph.D.), 1992, pp. 59-62.

which raises doubt about the application of the procedure prescribed by the *sūtra*.

3. *Nirṇaya* — This refers to the deliberation and the decision in case of doubt raised before, for example, *vārttika* 2 on 6.3.66, namely, *siddham tu harsvāntasya mumvacanāt* which answers the doubt.

4. *Vyākhyāviśeṣa* — This refers to different explanations that are possible of a particular word of the *sūtra*, for example, *vārttikas*, 1, 2 and 3 on 5.2.48 which explain the word *pūraṇa*.

5-6. *Gurulāghava* — This refers to the suggestion of brevity over prolixity found in the *sūtra*, for example, *vārttika* 5 on 6.3.9, namely, *ako'kta iti vā saṁdhyakṣarārtham* which proposes the brief reading *ako'kta* in place of long *haladantāt*.

7. *Kṛtavyudāsa* — This refers to the declaration of the portion of the *sūtra* as redundant or superfluous, for example, *vārttika* 1 on 1.1.34, namely, *avarādīnām ca punaḥ sūtrapāṭhe grahaṇānarthakyam gaṇe paṭhitatvāt*, which states that the use of the word *avara*, etc., in the *sūtra* is redundant because it is already stated in the *gaṇapāṭha*.

8. *Akṛtaśāsana* — This refers to the additions of various types to the *sūtras* of P which have been left uncovered, for example, *vārttika* 1 on 3.1.96, namely, *kelimara upasaṁkhyānam* which adds the suffix *kelimar* in the list of *kṛtya* suffixes.

The first seven features constitute the *uktacintā* aspect of the *vārttika*. The eighth one deals with the *anuktacintā* aspect. All the *upasaṁkhyāna* kind of *vārttikas* fall under the category of *anuktacintā*. As far as the *duruktacintā* is concerned, there is difference of opinion amongst scholars regarding the type itself.

Now, let us try to highlight a few most significant contributions made by K.

Philosophy in General

The contribution of K, in this regard, is to correlate the grammatical procedural technique with the theories propounded by different schools of thought of Indian philosophy. In this regard, I will cite one very important example:

kāryavipariṇāmād vā siddham.[7]

This *vārttika* appears in the discussion of the *sthānivadbhāva* on the *sūtra* 1.1.56. It is stated in the context of the *śabdanityatva* (permanency of the word). The *mahābhāṣyakāra* Patañjali elaborately discussed the issue. Here, I quote the views of Joshi and Roodbergen. They say — the term *kāryavipariṇāma* is rather immediately reminiscent of the Sāṅkhya doctrine called *satkāryavāda* of *pariṇāmavāda*.[8] They further say — "This doctrine lends itself admirably to support the *nityatva* of anything, whatsover. What is, cannot be destroyed and what is not, cannot come into being. Or, more precisely, the theory holds that the effect (*kārya*) is not something new coming into existence because it pre-exists in its cause in a latent form. It is merely a different manifestation of the cause.

On the basis of the validity of the above argument one can safely conclude that it is K who, for the first time, brings in the material from different schools of thoughts in the interpretation of the *sūtra*s of the Aṣṭādhyāyī.

7. Joshi and Roodbergen, *Sthānivadbhāvāhnika*, Part I, BORI, 1990, p. 17 of the text.

8. *Ibid.*, p. 80.

Philosophy of Language

The incorporation of the element of the philosophy of language must be stated as the prime contribution of K to the grammar of P. It was he, for the first time, in the tradition who interpreted the difficult words in the A which had philosophical leanings in an elaborate manner. It was he who introduced discussions on subtle matters of philosophy in the system of grammar which was restricted to the pure approach of derivational system by P.

Several instances can be cited, in this regard. However, we confine ourselves to only a few and the most important amongst them are detailed below.

WORD PERMANENCY

Indeed, it is K, for the first time, mentioned about the issue of the permanency of the speech element. Thus, it is in the third *āhnika* of the *Mbh*, K himself calls in question the method in which the technical term, namely, *vṛddhi* is preached by P and promptly solves this problem by the *vārttika* namely *siddham tu nityaśabdtvāt*[9] (the term *vṛddhi* can be established because the word is permanent). We find K raising such doubts many times and solving them with the same answer. What he means by the word permanency, in this regard, can be a matter of debate. Apparently, it seems that he is not referring to any doctrine of *buddhistha śabda* but rather to the fact that the relationship between a word and its meaning is already established in the language and the grammar proceeds from this fact. It does not creat this relation anew.

Whatever can be said to be the meaning of this "permanency" it cannot be denied that K can be said to be the

9. *Mahābhāṣya* of Patañjali, Nirnayasagar Press, Mumbai, 1932, Vol. I, p. 149.

first author of the tradition of the grammar of the P to have mentioned this important issue which got developed in the course of time into a full-fledged doctrine of *śabdanityavāda* which was identified as the contribution of grammarians in the overall field of the Indian philosophy.

RELATION BETWEEN GRAMMAR AND THE USAGE

Further, there appears a *vārttika* in the Paspśāhnika, namely, *siddhe śabdārthasambandhe lokatorthaprayukte śabdaprayoge śāstreṇa dharmaniyamaḥ*. This means "when (it is assumed that) the relation between a word and its meaning has already been established on account of the usage of people when (it is assumed that) the use of words is occasioned by the thing meant, grammar provides a restriction (on the use of words) for the sake of *dharma* 'religious merit' ", like in (the case of precepts) found in *loka* "non-ritual literature" and in the Veda.[10] This *vārttika* is the one which has been the soul basis of the arguments made by the later school of grammarians concerning the relationship of language and grammar. Indeed, this *vārttika* makes the position of the grammarians and for that matter of the ancient Indian thinkers as a whole about the exact nature and scope of grammar. The standpoint, taken by K, is indeed the most practical and groundbreaking. According to this standpoint, the basic purpose of grammar is to present the already existent data in systematic manner so as to cause the restriction in accruing merit and demerit. The implications of the *vārttika* are that

- the science of grammar does not produce words.
- it presumes the established relationship between the word and its meaning.

---

10. See Joshi and Roodbergen, Paspaśāhnika, Introduction, text, translation and notes, University of Poona, Pune, 1986, pp. 90, 115, 117, 120.

- The purpose of grammar is restriction.

ROLE OF SCIENCE

Further, this position of K is repeated in several *vārttikas* when he says *kimartham śāstram iti cet nivartakatvāt siddham* which underlines the purpose of a science of grammar and that is to restrict the application for merit. Indeed, if we look at this *vārttika* afresh, we find that this *vārttika* codifies the rules regarding the role of a science related not only to grammar but for that matter for all the sciences as such which exist in the universe. In other words, the principle stated by K can be applied for all the sciences of the universe. This principle implies that all sciences assume some existence at the very outset and then they proceed. They proceed to show restricted (and concentrated) applications of the codifications of the rules of the behaviour of certain elements under study and observation. This highlights the universality of the statements of K.

This statement also underlines the approach of K towards any system of knowledge. In this statement are hidden the moral undertones which proclaim that any science must not be developed for the sake of only development concern but there should also be a thought behind it about its proper application from the moral point of view. This approach might enlighten the global policy makers today as far as the nuclear technology is concerned. India is following the path, perhaps, which is reflected in these words of K.

In this regard the statement of the *Mbh* namely *samānāyām arthāvagatau śabdaiś cāpaśabdaiśca śāstreṇa dharmaniyamaḥ* (which means "Even though the process of understanding of the meaning from both a correct word and an incorrect word is similar, the science of grammar is for the sake of the restriction about merit") is worthwhile studying.

DEFINITION OF SENTENCE

Another most important contribution of the genius of K is the definition of the sentence that he provides which has become the landmark not only in the field of grammar but also in the history of sciences in India. This definition has earned him the title *vākyakāra*. Thus we find in the Samarthāhnika[11] the definition namely *ākhyātam sāvyayam sakārakam saviśeṣaṇam vākyam* (which means — the verbal form along with the indeclinable, the *kāraka*s and the other qualifiers is called a *vākya*) and *ektaiṅ vākyam* (that is a *vākya* which contains at least one verb). These two *vārttika*s imply that the essential part of a sentence is the verb in it. A sentence cannot be called complete if it is without a verb. The whole sentence revolves round the verb. P uses the word *vākya* in one of his *sūtras*[12] but he does not define it. It is then K who rightly comes forward and defines a sentence. It can be said that the theory of later grammarians that in a sentence-meaning, the meaning of the verbal form is the main component, can have the origins in this definitions of K.

Metalanguage of P

It is K, for the first time, who comments on the metalanguage of P. He also tries to formulate some rules regarding this metalanguage. Thus, he says *ikśtipau dhātunirdeśe* (which means while mentioning the verbal roots) P uses *ik* or the *śtip* for of that root. This explains words like *bhavateḥ* and *dhāreḥ* in *sūtra*s like *bhavateraḥ* (7.4.73) and *dhārer uttamarṇaḥ,* (1.4.35) respectively.

Elliptical Compound

The concept of this type of compounds is a major contribution of K. Traditionally, these are called *śākapārthivādi* compounds.

---

11. See Joshi and Roodbergen, Samarthāhnika, text, p. 17.

12. P. 8.1.8; 8.2.82.

Methods of Interpreting P

The method of *Yogavibhāga* which is so effectively employed by the later grammarians in interpreting the *sūtras* of P is seen first used by K. Thus, on 1.1.12 we find K resorting to this method which suggests to split the *sūtra* into two parts, namely, *adaso* and *māt* by the *vārttika yogavibhāgādvā*. Many such instances occur where K suggests to split the *sūtra*. The main purpose for resorting to this technique is an effort on the part of K to accommodate the newly found data in the existing system of the Aṣṭādhyāyī.

Another method which can be said to have been mentioned first by K is *jñāpaka* method. Thus, we find a *vārttika* on 1.1.50, namely, *bhrātuṣputragrahaṇam jñāpakam ekadeśanimittāt ṣatvapratiṣedhasya*. This *vārttika* presupposes that there exists a word *bhrātuṣputra* in the *kaskādigaṇa* and on the basis of that says that since there is mention of this word in the *kaskādigaṇa* there is no retroflex of *s* if it appears after an *ekadeśa*.

Conclusion

From the foregone discussion, one can conclude, safely, that, indeed K gave the system of grammar developed by P, a fresh philosophical basis and the outlook and the background which, no other system of Sanskrit grammar seems to have had. It, thus, enriched the already existing excellence of P's grammar and supported it from a different point of view, viz., philosophy. Indeed K can be considered as one of the greats, India ever produced.

References

PRIMARY SOURCES

The Aṣṭādhyāyī of Pāṇini, Ed. Böhtlingk, 1877.

The Mahābhāṣya of Patañjali, Nirnayasagar Press, Mumbai, 1932, Vol. I.

The Mahābhāṣya of Patañjali, Paspaśāhnika, Introduction, text, translation and notes, University of Poona, Pune, 1986.

The Mahābhāṣya of Patañjali, The Samarthāhnika, Joshi and Roodbergen, Center of Advanced Study of Sanskrit, University of Pune, 1968.

The Mahābhāṣya of Patañjali, The Sthānivadbhāvāhnika, Part I, Joshi and Roodbergen, BORI, 1990.

Pārāśaropapurāṇa, Ed. Kapildev Tripathy, Sampurnananda Sanskrit Visvavidyalaya, Vārāṇasī, 1990.

SECONDARY SOURCES

Cardona, G., *Pāṇini: A Survey of Research*, Motilal Banarsidass, New Delhi, 1974.

Cardona, G., *Recent Researches in Pāṇinian Studies*, Motial Banarsidass, 1998.

Laddu, S.D., *Evolution of Sanskrit Language from Pāṇini to Patañjali*, CASS, University of Pune, Pune, 1967.

Mishra, Vedapati, *Vyākaraṇavārttika: eka samīkṣātmaka adhyayana* (in Hindi), Prithivi Prakashan, Vārāṇasī, 1970.

Mishra, Madhusudan, *Critical Study of the Vārttikas of Kātyāyana* (A dissertation submitted to the University of Pune for the degree of Ph.D.), 1992.

Paranjape, V.G., *Le vārttika de Kātyāyana: une etude du style, du vocabulaire et des postulats philosophiques*, Weissche, Universitat buchh und lung, Heidelberg, 1922.

Proceedings of the National seminar on the sentence and sentence meaning, edited by Dr. S.D. Joshi and Dr. S.D. Laddu, CASS, University of Pune, Pune, 1981.

Pt. Yudhiṣṭhira Mīmāṁsaka, *Saṁskṛta Vyākaraṇa śāstra kā itihāsa*, Ramlal Kapur Trust, Bahalgarh, Sonepat, Haryana, 1971, Vol. I.

7

Patañjali, The Bhāṣyakāra*

Saroja Bhate

ONCE Lord Viṣṇu, while relaxing in his bed of Śeṣa, the divine serpent, was interestingly watching the *tāṇḍava* dance of Lord Śiva. Śeṣa, who felt the heavy weight of Viṣṇu on account of his total engrossment in the dance, expressed to his Lord his genuine desire to get a chance to watch the ecstatic divine dance. Viṣṇu immediately consented and told him that he would be reborn on the earth and would get a chance to enjoy the spectacle of Śiva's dance. Śeṣa was, accordingly, reborn as a divine child falling in the hallowed hands of Goṇikā, a woman ascetic while she was offering *arghya* to the Sun. Goṇikā accepted the child and gave him a significant name, Patañjali (*patat* "falling", *añjali* "hallowed hands"). The child went to a forest to practice penance in order to propitiate Śiva. Many years passed and finally Śiva, pleased with the penance of the divine child, granted him the boon to witness the spectacle of his divine dance. Śiva further asked him (the child) to write a commentary on Pāṇini's grammar and teach the same to his desciples. Patañjali agreed and he started both composing a *bhāṣya* and began teaching students. Being an incarnation of Śeṣa with 1000 heads, Patañjali could, simultaneously, explain difficulties of his students with his multiple mouths. He used

---

* I am extremly thankful to my friend Mr. Vincenzo Vergiani, who read the draft of this article and made valuable suggestions.

to hide himself behind a curtain while teaching so that the students were not dazed by the glare of his 1000 heads. However, one day, the students, unable to resist anymore their curiosity to see the face of their *guru*, raised the curtain and were, instantaneously, burnt and reduced to ashes. The only one left behind was a student who had gone out at that time. Patañjali taught him the whole *bhāṣya* which was further transmitted by him to his disciples.[1]

This is the traditional account of Patañjali's life recorded in some books of history. According to another account, a divine child fell into the hands of a sage in Gonarda country who gave him the name Patañjali, accepting him as his own child and, later, Patañjali wrote his *Mahābhāṣya* as an extended version of the *laghubhāṣya,* composed by this sage.[2] We do not get any other information about Patañjali's life and times. The above stories are, perhaps, based on the references to words like *Gonardīya* and *Goṇikāputra* found in the *Vyākaraṇa-mahābhāṣya*. According to the generally accepted opinion, Patañjali lived, sometime around 150 BC during the reign of Puṣyamitra Śuṅga, the founder of Śuṅga dynasty.[3] There is, however, no unanimity among the scholars regarding his place of birth and residence. H. Scharfe is, for instance, of the opinion that Patañjali lived in Mathurā which is, often, mentioned by him or a place nearby.[4] George Cardona has summed up views of different scholars without noting his agreement to anyone

---

1. See *Śrīmadbhāgavatapatañjalikṛta Vyākaraṇamahābhāṣya* with Marāṭhī translation by M.M. Vasudevashastri Abhyankar, Deccan Education Society, Pune, 1954, Vol. VII, pp. 349-50.
2. *Ibid*. p. 71.
3. Hartmut Scharfe, *A History of Indian Literature, Grammatical Literature,* Ed. J. Gonda, Otto Harrasowitz, Wiesbaden, 1977, p. 153.
4. *Ibid*.

of them.[5] Thus, for instance, he refers to the view of R.G. Bhandarkar, namely, that Patañjali came from an area north by north-west of Oudh (Ayodhyā). Since Patañjali describes Kātyāyana at one place as *dākṣiṇātya*, it is likely that he lived, somewhere, in the north.

The last *muni* in the *Trimunivyākaraṇa* tradition, Patañjali exercised a great influence on the Pāṇinian tradition, as is evinced by the *paribhāṣā*, *yathottaraṁ munīnāṁ prāmāṇyam* "the authority of the sages (Pāṇini, Kātyāyana and Patañjali) is in the ascending order (of their time of existence)". The later Pāṇinian tradition is often found turning to Patañjali's *Vyākaraṇamahābhāṣya* not only for seeking help in interpreting Pāṇini but also for rules and methodology of interpretation. The post-*trimuni* development of the Pāṇinian school, including its branches of philosophy and semantics, has the *Mahābhāṣya* as its foundation. The *Mahābhāṣya*, thus, appears as a keystone of the whole grammatical structure, based on Pāṇini. Nāgojībhaṭṭa, the last star in the galaxy of the Pāṇinian *Vaiyākaraṇa*s, sometimes, remarks in connection with a solution to a problem, *siddhyatyevaṁ bhāṣyaviruddhaṁ tu bhavati* that "it may be accomplished in this way, but it goes against the *bhāṣya* (and, hence, it is not acceptable)." So strong was the impact of Patañjali's words on the grammarians, who followed him, that they were not willing to accept even that which was right and proper if it went against his view. References to Patañjali and citations from his *bhāṣya* scattered throughout the grammatical literature as statements from an infallible authority speak for the place of veneration and respect, enjoyed by Patañjali in the history of the science of language in India.

To what does Patañjali owe this central position in the Pāṇinian tradition?

---

5. George Cardona, *Pāṇini: A Survey of Research*, Motilal Banarsidass, Delhi, First Indian Reprint 1980, p. 269.

An attempt is made in what follows to highlight some of the salient featuress of Patañjali's work.

The *Vyākaraṇamahābhāṣya,* written by Patañjali, belongs to a type of commentary, called *bhāṣya*. Traditionally, a *bhāṣya* explains the meaning of the *sūtra,* following the words in it, and, further, discusses the words it uses to explain the meaning.[6]

This, however, is not a satisfactory definition. A *bhāṣya* is something more than a mere elucidation; it includes discussion on different topics. Moreover, according to one scholar the term *bhāṣya* implies the use of *bhāṣā* "simple language."[7] The *Mahābhāṣya* of Patañjali goes beyond these fixed notions and stands by itself in the whole range of Sanskrit grammatical literature. It is true that it strikes a modern student of grammar, at the outset, as an incomplete commentary. In fact, it is primarily a commentary on the *Vārttika*s of Kātyāyana, and hence, confined to a little more than one-third of the *Aṣṭādhyāyī*. Very few among the 1713 *sūtras* discussed in the *Bhāṣya* are treated by Patañjali independently of the *Varttika*s. The aim of Patañjali agrees with that of Kātyāyana which consists in testing the validity of the Pāṇinian *sūtra*s. Following Kātyāyana, Patañjali discusses the wording of the *sūtra*s (traditionally known as *padakṛtya*). In addition, he tries to relate the *śāstra* (theory) to *prayoga* (practice), draws correspondences from parallel disciplines and, sometimes, takes certain grammatical concepts to metaphysical heights. His approach,

---

6. सूत्रार्थो वर्ण्यते यत्र पदैः सूत्रानुकारिभिः
स्वपदानि च वर्ण्यन्ते भाष्यं भाष्यविदो विदुः ॥

(*Parāśara Purāṇa*, XVIII.15 quoted in the *Dictionary of Sanskrit Grammar* by V.K. Abhyankar and J.M. Shukla, Oriental Institute, Baroda (1977).

7. Hartmut Scharfe, *A History of Indian Literature, Grammatical Literature*, Wiesbaden, 1977, p. 152.

thus, covers the whole range of issues from philology to philosophy of language. Because of the extensive character of his treatment of the words of his two masters, Patañjali's work has grown in size. Kaiyaṭa, his commentator, rightly describes his work as *bhāṣyābdhi* "ocean in the form of *bhāṣya*." This robust look must have been one of the factors responsible for its popularity throughout the history of the Indian grammatical tradition. Patañjali owes respect also to the fact that his work represents the earliest attempt to recapitulate the essentials of the science of the language from the centuries of the debate preceding him and arrange them in the form of a compendium. Here, the grammarians, who followed Patañjali, found solutions to most of their problems of interpreting Pāṇini. The *Bhāṣya* appeared as a valuable aid in understanding the terse *sūtra*s and teaching them to students. It was looked with greater importance because of the pioneering efforts of the *bhāṣyakāra* in fixing the fundamental text of Sanskrit grammar, Pāṇini's *Aṣṭādhyāyī* as well as Kātyāyana's *Vārttikas*. It appears from some of Patañjali's remarks that the *Sūtrapāṭha*, that was orally transmitted, was in a floating stage with variations in the wording, at least, of some *sūtra*s. Patañjali was, perhaps, the foremost teacher to pin them down and fix the text for posteriority. Apart from this philological contribution, Patañjali can be credited with reintroducing Vyākaraṇa as an indispensable subject in the curriculum of Indian education of the past. The opening passage of the Paspaśāhnika, listing purposes of the study of Vyākaraṇa, shows how Patañjali puts his marketing skill to test to convince his disciples of the utility of Vyākaraṇa not only for a student but also for common man. The purposes enlisted by him range between earthly achievements like oral skills and personality development and transcendental attainments like union with the highest reality. It must be admitted that Patañjali's efforts to advocate the importance of grammar have borne fruit since grammar has been, through the centuries, a compulsory component of the syllabi in Sanskrit *pāṭhaśālā*s in greater India.

While, on the one hand, Indian scientific tradition is indebted to Patañjali for recording the progress of speculations in science, including a number of branches like physics, logic, and metaphysics, on the other, for students of history his work stands as a valuable document of the state of the art in diverse aspects of Indian culture such as literature, arts and crafts. Several scholars have tried to collect information on realia reflected in the *Bhāṣya*, K.V. Abhyankar remarks, for instance, that "There were prevalent in the days of Patañjali all the three representation of past events . . . the dramatical, the pictorial and the verbal. . . ."[8] Much more still needs to be done to reconstruct the history of Indian linguistics on the basis of the linguistic speculations, scatterred throughout the *Bhāṣya*. Patañjali's singular contribution is not, however, confined to the transmission of the earlier cultural material. It serves both as a database and a knowledge base though in a restricted sense. Apart from preserving the cultural data, Patañjali has initiated efforts in search of new methods of interpretation. In addition to the use of the tools of interpretation traditionally handed down to him, he offers ad hoc solutions to many a problem arising at the time of understanding and implementing Pāṇini's *sūtras*. Later, Pāṇinian tradition has collected such solutions and formalized them in the form of generalized rules of interpretation, called *paribhāṣā*s. A striking feature of these *paribhāṣā*s is their close affinity with the popular maxims.

The well-known maxim of the cancellation of *utsarga* "general rule" by *apavāda* "special rule" is, for instance, explained with the help of a popular illustration in the *Bhāṣya* as follows:

8. K.V. Abhyankar, ed. *Patañjali's Vyākaraṇa — Mahābhāṣya*, 7 vols., Deccan Education Society, Poona, 1938-54.

naiveśvara ājñāpayati nāpi dharmasūtrakārāḥ paṭhanti apavādairutsargā bādhyantām iti । *kintarhi* । *laukiko'yaṁ dṛṣṭāntaḥ* । *loke hi satyapi sambhave bādhanaṁ bhavati* । *tadyathā dadhi brāhmaṇebhyo dīyatāṁ takraṁ kauṇḍinyāyeti satyapi sambhave dadhidānasya takradānaṁ nivartakaṁ bhavati* ।[9]

Neither does the god order nor do authors of Dharmasūtra read, "general rules should be cancelled by particular rules." "What then?" This is a popular illustration. In the society there is cancellation (of a rule) even when there exists possibility (of its) application. For instance, (it is said), "Give curds to Brahmins and buttermilk to Kaundinya." Here, in spite of the possibility of giving curds (to Kaundinya), giving of buttermilk (to him) returns (the act of) giving curds.

The *Mahābhāṣya* is teeming with such references to popular maxims. It has initiated the attempt to bridge the gap between *śāstra* and *loka*.

All these merits of the *Mahābhāṣya*, beautifully summed up by Bhartṛhari at the end of the second book of the *Vākyapadīya*[10], however, proved fatal to the continuation of the tradition of the study of the *Bhāṣya*. As recorded by Bhartṛhari, both the immense expanse and unfathomable depth of this text were out of reach for unmotivated and dull students as a result of which the tradition was lost. However, the only manuscript preserved somewhere in the south was studied and transmitted by Candrācārya from whom Bhartṛhari's *guru* received instruction. Bhartṛhari thus claims to have contributed to the

9. See *Vyākaraṇamahābhāṣya*, ed. Vedavrat, Gurukul Jhajjiar, Vol. I, 1962, p. 352.

10. See the *Vākyapadīya of Bharatṛhari, Kāṇḍa*, II, Ed. K.A. Subramania Iyer, Motilal Banarsidass, Delhi, 1983, verses 476-82.

revival of the study of the *Bhāṣya*. We are, indeed, fortunate, thanks to Bhartṛhari, in having the complete text of the *Mahābhāṣya* preserved for us.

The most attractive feature of the *Bhāṣya* for a modern student is its language. It is both simple and beautiful. Like a rivulet it smoothly flows along through rocks and meadows of linguistic debates and discourses. Like evening breeze it rustles through the branches and leaves of arguments and discussions. Occasionally, it sends ripples of humour. Hardly does it engulf a reader in a whirlpool of stormy debates.

The mode of dialogue chosen for the discourse is yet another fascinating feature of the *Bhāṣya*. It is divided into 85 chapters, called *āhnika*s. It is believed on the basis of the term *āhnika* literally meaning, that which is accomplished during a day that the *Bhāṣya* constitutes a compilation of 85 classroom lectures, delivered by Patañjali during 85 days. And who were sitting in this class? Traditionally, each *āhnika* is a conversation among the teacher, the students, the teaching assistant (*ācāryadeśīya*) not as accomplished as the teacher and a fresh graduate who has partly digested the knowledge he has gained (*ekadeśin*). A closer look at these *āhnika*s, further, reveals that, at times, the discussion comes to close without a final judgement on a certain topic. Therefore, the *Bhāṣya* appears to be a testimony of a given stage in the development of the *śāstra* on Pāṇini's grammar, but it does not represent the final outcome of the debate. Although tradition respects it as the highest authority, the *Bhāṣya* indeed leaves many a grammatical issue unsettled and, hence, it is still controversial.

Be it as may, the Bhāṣya presents itself as a model of vibrant prose, throbbing with life. It is a unique example of a scientific discourse presented in the form of a tea-table discussion among cheerful participants. A couple of illustrations will prove the point. Following is a passage from the Paspaśāhnika, discussing the issue whether religious merit is obtained by knowledge of usage of correct words:

yadi prayoge dharmaḥ sarvo loko'bhyudayena yujyate ।
kaścedānīṁ bhavato matsaro yadi sarvo lokobhyudayana yujyate ॥
na khalu kaścitmatsaraḥ prayatnānarthakyaṁ to bhavati ।
phalavatā ca nāma prayatnena bhavitavyaṁ na ca prayatnaḥ phalād vyatirecyaḥ ॥
nanu ca ye kṛtaprayatnāste sādhīyaḥ śabdān prayokṣyante ta eva sādhīyo'bhyudayena yokṣyante ।
vyatireko pi vai lakṣyante dṛśyante hi kṛtaprayatnāścāpravīṇāḥ akṛtaprayatnāśca pravīṇāḥ tatra phalavyatireko pi syāt ।
evaṁ tarhi nāpi jñāna eva dharmo nāpi prayoge eva ।[11]

If religious merit (consists) in usage, everybody will be associated with well-being.

Why are you so jealous if everyone may be associated with well-being?

No question of being jealous. But then efforts (to use correct words) will be purposeless. An effort must, indeed, have a reward. No effort should be separated from fruit.

(Don't we see that) those who make efforts will be able to use words more correctly and, hence, they alone will be more suitably connected with well-being?

The contrary is also seen. Indeed, (we) see that those who make efforts are (still) not proficient and those who do not make efforts are (yet) efficient. Thus, there would be no agreement (between effort and) fruit.

11. *Vyākaraṇamabhāṣya Paspaśāhnika*, Ed. S.D. Joshi, p. 31.

In that case, (let us maintain that) religious merit consists neither in knowledge, alone, nor in usage, alone.

It will be clear from the above-quoted passage that the whole discussion takes place as a free conversation among friends. The language bears a colloquial touch. It is strikingly different from the artificial śāstric languages used by the later grammarians like Nāgojībhaṭṭa and Koṇḍabhaṭṭa. However, the youthful wit and humour never overpower the logical undercurrent of the discussion. Patañjali is a perfect master who maintains balance between the expression and the content. The dialectic reflected in the following passage from Paspaśāhnika shows Patañjali's skill in argumentation:

> *idam tāvat vipratiṣiddhaṁ yaducyate santi vai śabdāḥ aprayuktā iti । yadi santi nāprayuktā athāprayuktā na santi santi cāprayuktāśceti vipratiṣiddham । prayuñjāna eva khalu bhavānāha santi śabdā aprayuktā iti । kaścedānīmanyo bhavajjātīyakaḥ puruṣaḥ śabdānāṁ prayoge sādhuḥ syāt ।*
>
> *naitad vipratiṣiddham । santīti tāvat brūmo yalloke prayuktā iti । yadapyucyate kaścedānīmanyo bhavajjātiyakaḥ puruṣaḥ śabdānāṁ prayoge sādhuḥ syāditi na brūmo smābhiraprayuktā iti ।*
> *kiṁ tarhi*
> *loke prayuktāḥ ।*
> *namu ca bhavānapyabhyantaro loke ।*
> *abhayantaro haṁ loke natvahaṁ lokaḥ ।*[12]

- This is, indeed, contradictory to say. There are words which are not in use. If they are there, they cannot be (described as) not in use; if they are not in use, they are not there. There is a contradiction between they are there and they are not in use. Moreover, while

12. *Vyākaraṇamahābhāṣya Paspaśāhnika*, ed. S.D. Joshi.

using them you say that they are there but not in use. Which other person of your standing could be (regarded) corect in the matter of use of words?

- There is no contradiction. We do say that there are words since those who know the science (of grammar) prescribe them in accordance with the science (of grammar). (When) we say (that these words) are not in use (we mean that) they are not in use among people. And with reference to what you say, "Which other person of your standing could be (regarded) correct in the matter of use of words?" (my reply is), we do not say that they are not used by us.
- What then?
- They are not in use among the people.
- But are you not one among the people.
- I am included in the people, but I am not the people.

The free and unhampered flow of the dialogue in lively Sanskrit as illustrated by the above passage is characteristic of the *Bhāṣya*.

Was Patañjali's a spoken language? Some Indologists believe that Sanskrit had never been a spoken language, in the true sense. As the name *samskṛta* suggests, it was refined, artificially polished and embellished for use in specific areas like education and culture. It functioned as *lingua franca* as a link language through all the centuries of its history. We find support to this view in Patañjali's *bhāṣya*.[13] However, the language used by Patañjali has a more colloquial than formal appearance. It may not have been the spoken language in the sense of anybody's mother tongue or market language in his

13. Madhav Deshpande, *Sanskrit and Prākrit*.

time. But the flexibility with which it moves in diverse semantic areas, its richness of vocabulary and the wide area of usage covered by it make us believe that in Patañjali's time Sanskrit must have been freely and widely used almost as a spoken language, though in restricted circles. A good number of citations in the *Bhāṣya* from epics and poems also point to the prosperity of Sanskrit as a literary language. The prose of the *Bhāṣya* represents an important landmark in the history of the development of Sanskrit language.

A student of Patañjali is as much as deeply impressed by his sound logic as by his vigorous style. He, often, engages himself with the "why" of an issue rather than with the mere 'what'. The passages, quoted above, show the logical acumen with which he handles the issues. On a number of occasions, he offers alternative solutions. His arguments evince not only his insistence on reasoning but also his thorough acquaintance with the achievements of his forefathers in Vyākaraṇa as well as other branches of knowledge. He approaches grammatical statements of his predecessors from a variety of angles and discusses threadbare their implications. While following in the footsteps of Kātyāyana, Patañjali also considers repercussions of accepting or rejecting a rule or a *paribhāṣā*. The *sūtras* of Pāṇini are subjected to scrutiny from both grammatical and semantic point of view. His *Bhāṣya* on P.5.3.95 cited below is a good illustration of some of the features of his logic described above:

> *avakṣepaṇe kan vidhīyate kutsite kaḥ ka etayorarthayorviśeṣaḥ?*
>
> *avakṣepaṇaṁ karaṇaṁ kutsitaṁ karma* ।
>
> *avakṣepaṇaṁ vai kutsitaṁ karaṇaṁ tena yatkutsyate, tadapi kutsitaṁ bhavati* । *tatra kutsita ityeva siddhaṁ bhavati*
>
> *evaṁ tarhi yatparasya kutsārthamupādīyate tadihodāraṇam* ।
>
> *vyākaraṇakena namāyaṁ garvitaḥ yājnikyena nāmāyaṁ garvitaḥ* ।

yatsvakutsārthamupādīyate tattatrodāharaṇam devadattakaḥ yajñadattakaḥ

- (The suffix) *kan* is prescribed to convey despizing and the (suffix) *ka* is prescribed to convey (something) contemptuous. What is the difference between these two meanings?
- *avakṣepaṇa* denotes a means (of despizing) while *kutsita* denotes a (contemptuous) act.
- But *avakṣepaṇa*, the means (of despizing) is also contemptuous and that which is despised by means of it is also contemptuous. Thus, (both the purposes) will be served by (merely stating the rule) *kutsite* (i.e., *ka* is added to convey something contemptuous).
- In that case, that which is used to despise somebody is the example of this rule (i.e., *kan* is added to convey despizing): "He is conceited by the wretched grammar"; he is conceited by the wretched ritualism". That which is used to convey contempt of (the object signified by the stem) itself is an example of that rule (i.e., *ka* is added to convey contempt): "The wretched Devadatta, the wretched Yajñadatta.

The deep faith in the words of the Teacher, reflected in the above passage is the foundation of Patañjali's logic. His veneration for Pāṇini is expressed in the following passage:

> *pramāṇabhūta ācāryo darbhapavitrapāṇiḥ śucāvavakāśe prāṅmukha upviśya mahatā prayatnena sūtrāṇi praṇayati sma* I *tatrāśakhyaṁ varṇenāpyanarthakena bhavituṁ kiṁ punariyatā sūtreṇa* I[14]

Respected Teacher, the great authority, composed the

14. *Vyākaraṇamahābhāṣyam*, Ed. Vedavrata, Gurukula, Jhajjar, Vol. I, 1962, p. 128.

> *sūtras* with great effort while sitting in a holy place, facing the east and with his hand purified by (holding) *darbha* (grass). Therefore, it is impossible even for a single letter to be purposeless, for less for a *sūtra* of this (length).

This ardent faith in the master does not, however, make Patañjali blind to his shortcomings. He does not hesitate, for instance, to express his inability to justify a certain *sūtra* or a word, thereof. He has, in fact, recommended rejection of some *sūtras* either because they are redundant or because they fail to fulfil the purpose of explaining certain usage. How to account for this ambivalence? We must try to understand Patañjali with the help of the given text. As it appears, Patañjali rejects a certain expression or *sūtra* only after weighing its pros and cons. He makes every attempt to relate the *sūtra* to the facts of language. But he is not successful, every time, obviously, because there is a gap of three or four centuries between him and Pāṇini. If we accept that the *āhnikas* are classroom lectures, we can understand the message Patañjali wants to convey to his students, through his expression of deep veneration to Pāṇini, who could not have uttered a single meaningless phoneme: Take Pāṇini seriously; try to under stand the deeper meaning of his pronouncements; think hundred times before you find fault with this profound Teacher.

Yet another case of Patañjali's apparent ambivalence is his general outlook on Vyākaraṇa as a component of education. After firmly establishing in the Paspaśāhnika the utility of the study of Vyākaraṇa for the life on this planet as well as in the other world, Patañjali proceeds to examine the relevance of Pāṇini's *Aṣṭādhyāyī*. He has taken up the issue as an incidental point in the course of his discussions and has given a candid expression to his views on grammar. While discussing

P.6.3.109, for instance, Patañjali initiates discussion on the relation between language and grammar and sums up by declaring that the usage of the *śiṣṭas*, the elites, is the authority for correct words. If one can learn correct words by observing the usage of the *śiṣṭas* why should one study the grammar, the *Aṣṭādhyāyī*? Prompt is the reply from Patañjali: *śiṣṭaparijñānārthā aṣṭādhyāyī*, "*Aṣṭādhyāyī* is meant (to enable you) to recognize the *śiṣṭas*." The purpose of the study of grammar is relegated to a still lower level in the *Bhāṣya* on P.1.2.32. Here, Patañjali begins with a tall claim about the worth of Vyākaraṇa by announcing, *vyākaraṇaṁ nāmeyam uttarā vidyā* "Grammar indeed is a great lore" and ends up with a realization, *anvākhyāna-mevedaṁ tarhi mandabuddhe*, "It is, then, an instruction for the sake of the dull-witted." The whole paraphernalia of his arguments, accompanied by the sacred utterances in support of the high value of the study of grammar in the *Paspaśāhnika*, appears, therefore, more or less, as a ritual service to the God of Word, to whom Patañjali is committed.

How does Patañjali appeal to a modern student with no emotional involvement in grammar and with commitment to reasoning alone? Out of his magnificent masterpiece, Patañjali emerges as a magnanimous personality, an erudite scholar, an ideal and spirited teacher, an unassuming learned master with a delightful outlook, who looks far beyond the philology of the subject, chosen by him, transcends the boundaries of Vyākaraṇa and exalts his students to the realm of metaphysics by bringing learning closer to the pure aesthetic delight. His valuable contributions to Indian semantics and philosophy of language as well as to Indian linguistics such as his views on the eternal language, the *sphoṭa*, form the subject-matter of a separate article. His *Mahābhāṣya*, like a treasure-cave is awaiting arrival of an Alibābā who knows the *mantra* of "open sesame" and enters the brilliant inside to take away the dazzling gems of thought.

8

Date of Patañjali: A Review

Jatindramohan Mishra

AMONG the large number of commentaries on the *Aṣṭādhyāyī*, none excels Patañjali's effort in the sureness of the critical touch and in the impeachability of the authority. Written in a language which is rendered almost unique by the combination of simplicity and vigour and consisting mainly of dialogues, which impart to it an absorbing interest, saving it from the dryness that usually characterizes a śāstric commentary, the *Mahābhāṣya* stands out from the rest of its kind, deserving richly the esteem in which it has always been held as an invaluable commentary. An important feature of the work is that it explains many rigid and recondite śāstric rules in terms of maxims derived from everyday life, which makes it higher and under that a śāstric commentary and enables it to throw a flood of light on the religious, social and other various aspects of contemporary life. That is why, it becomes an important issue to fix Patañjali's date, depending upon which the ancient Indian history can be reviewed and it can give a new dimension to the study of Indology.

Though Patañjali's authorship, traditionally, claims over three different texts,[1] the same authorship is debatable. So,

---

1. योगेन चित्तस्य पदेन वाचां मलं शरीरस्थ च वैद्यकेन।
योऽपाकरोत्तं प्रवरं मुनीनां पतञ्जलिं प्राञ्जलेरानतोऽस्मि॥

not going in details into the controversy, the present article aims at reviewing the discussions, made by the scholars over a couple of centuries, on the date of Patañjali, who is the author of *Mahābhāṣya*. Here, views of some prominent scholars are discussed and reviewed, critically.

Prof. Theodor Goldstücker[2]

Before presenting his own view, Prof. Goldstücker briefly analyses Prof. Max Müller, viewing in this regard. Prof. Müller says, "It is impossible to say at what time, the *Mahābhāṣya* was first composed." Saying this, he might be referring to Kalhaṇa's *Rājtaraṅgiṇī*, that it was re-composed by Candrācārya, being inspired by the king Abhimanyu, Müller says, "Patañjali is, sometimes, identified with Piṅgala and on this view, as Piṅgala is called the younger brother of Pāṇini or, at least, the descendant of Pāṇini, it might be supposed that the original composition of the *Mahābhāṣya* belonged to the third century BC. But the identity of Piṅgala and Patañjali is far from probable and it would be rash to use it as a foundation for other calculations." "This is the only date, the fixing of which is called impossible in Müller's 'Ancient Sanskrit Literature'", thus, opines Prof. Goldstücker.

He gives a reference to *Mahābhāṣya*'s explanation on the rule *jīvikārthe cāpaṇye*,[3] which hints that Patañjali didn't live

---

A verse is indicating Patañjali's authorship in texts, 1. *Yogasūtra*, 2. *Vyākaraṇa Śāstra*, 3. A text related to Medicine. This is quoted from the first notes of B.N. Puri in the book, *India in the Time of Patañjali*, p. 14.

2. Here is the summarization of what Prof. Theodor Goldstücker has stated in the book *Paṇini*, published at the Chowkhamba Sanskrit Series Office, Vārāṇasī (1965), pp. 247-58.

3. जीविकार्थे चापण्ये (P. 5.3.99). *Bhāṣya* — "अपण्य इत्युच्यते तत्रेदं न सिद्धयति। शिवः स्कन्दो विशाख इति। किं कारणम्।मौर्यैर्हिरण्यार्थिभिरर्चाः प्रकल्पिताः। भवेत्। तासु न स्यात्। यास्त्वेताः सम्प्रतिपूजार्थाः तासु भविष्यति।

before the first king of Maurya, i.e., Candragupta, who ruled by 315 BC, as the history fixes the time. Having closer view of the wordings of the *Mahābhāṣya*, Goldstücker reaches at the point that Patañjali lived after the fall of Maurya dynasty, i.e., 180 BC.

To support his view, he also compares with another rule explained by Patañjali, i.e., *anadyatane laṅ* (3-2-111). On this rule, there is a *vārttika*, i.e., *parokṣe ca lokavijñāte prayokrur-darśanavijaye*, which means, when the fact, related is out of sight and notorious, but could be seen by the person who uses the verb *laṅ* can also be applied there. To illustrate, Patañjali says, *aruṇadyavanaḥ sāketam* and *aruṇadyavano mādhyamikān*.[4] It means, Yavana besieged Sāketa (now Ayodhyā) and Mādhyamikas. Nāgeśa[5] in his commentary *Uddyota* on the *Mahābhāṣya* says, the fact has happened when Patañjali lived, though he was not on the spot.

Now Mādhyamika is a well-known sect in Buddhism which was founded by Nāgārjuna whose period is traditionally taken to be after 400 years (according to the northern Buddhists) and 500 years (according to the southern Buddhists) of

---

Here, the word 'मौर्य' indicates that Patañjali should be after मौर्य, i.e., at least, after first Maurya king, Candragupta.

This reference is from the footnote no. 266, p. 248 of the book *Paṇini* of T. Golddtücker, Chowkhamba Sanskrit Series Office, Vārāṇasī (1965).

4. माध्यमिकान् variant readings are found as माध्यमिकान् and माध्यमिकाम्। The earlier would mean "to the Mādhyamikas, i.e., the people of the Mādhyamika sect" and the later would mean "to the city, viz., माध्यमिका". However this does not affect in the calculation of the date.

5. Nāgeśa in his commentary *Uddyota* says "भाष्ये जघान इति किम्। स बधो हि नेदानीन्तनप्रयोक्तुर्दर्शनयोग्यः। अरुणदित्युदाहरणे तु तुल्यकालः प्रवर्तत इति बोध्यः। (on *Bhāṣya* 3.2.111). Reference is from footnote no. 267, pp. 249-50, of the book, *Pāṇini* by T. Goldstücker.

Buddha's death. If the date of Buddha's death is 543 BC (as Prof. Lassen defines) and Nāgārjuna 400 years after that, then it is 143 BC, when Nāgārjuna and Patañjali, both lived. So *Mahābhāṣya* should have been composed in between 140 BC and 120 BC. More certainly, it can only be Menandars among the Yavana king, who had attacked Ayodhyā. Because there is a coin found at Mathurā, blocked with his image. Menander extended his conquests as far as the Yamunā river. According to Prof. Lassen's researches, more than 20 years from about 144 BC, he reigned.

Prof. R.G. Bhandarkar[6]

After analysing Prof. Goldstücker's views, Prof. Bhandarkar supplements another strong point which makes the calculations more accurate. Along with all the references Prof. Goldstücker has made, Prof. Bhandarkar notices another clue, i.e., on the rule *vartamāne laṭ* (3-2-123), the *Vārttika* — *pravṛttasyāvirāme śiṣyā bhavantyavartmānatvāt*. This means, the rule should be made teaching the use of present tense (*laṭ*) to denote an action or undertaking which has begun, but not finished. Patañjali, for this, illustrates, *iha puṣpamitraṁ*[7] *yājayāmaḥ*, which indicates that Patañjali must have lived at the time of Puṣpamitra. Prof. Bhandarkar, says, "this cannot be an imaginary instance for such a one would not bring out the distinctive sense that Patañjali wishes to convey, viz., that the action has begun but not ended." Moreover, when a great text mentions somebody's

6. Here is the gist of Prof. R.G. Bhandarkar in the article viz., "On the Date of Patañjali and the king in whose reign he lived" in the book *A Reader on the Sanskrit Grammarians*, Ed. by J.F. Staal, The MIT Press, Cambridge, Massachusetts and London, England, 1972, pp. 78-81.

7. Variant reading are found as पुष्पमित्र and पुष्यमित्र. Perhaps, this is because of the resemblance of the two letters य & प. However, calculation of the period is not affected by this problem.

name, he must be a great personality, such as a king who employed priests to perform the great sacrifice for him. In the older days, it was Indian kings that propitiated the gods and patronized the brāhmaṇas in this way.

Further, Prof. Bhandarkar reaches with the fact that Puṣyamitra was the king of Pāṭaliputra, the capital of Magadha, which was the most powerful kingdom during a few centuries before Christ and the sovereigns of which extended their sway over a large portion of India. Patañjali, quite often, mentions Pāṭaliputra, which indicates that he had a great deal to do with Pāṭaliputra or, at least, he lived there for some period. On that account, the city and things, concerning it, were uppermost in his thought. This inference is strengthened with co-reference of Candragupta, the Maurya king of Magadha.

Purāṇas also support the view that there was only one king of Magadha, named Puṣyamitra, the founder of Śuṅga dynasty, which succeeded the Mauryas. Puṣyamitra was the commander-in-chief of Bṛhadratha, the last Maurya king, who usurped the throne after having killed his master.

The ten Mauryas are said to have ruled the kingdom for 137 years. The accession of Candragupta, the first of these ten, has been fixed at about 315 BC. Puṣyamitra, therefore, must have raised himself to the throne at about 178 BC. The *Matsya Purāṇa* assigns him a reign of 36 years, i.e., from 178 BC to 142 BC. It follows then that Patañjali wrote his comments on Pān-3-2-123 *vartamāne laṭ*, sometimes, between these limits.

Thus, there is not a big difference between Prof. Goldstücker and Prof. Bhandarkar. Goldstücker accepts the period of *Mahābhāṣya* to be from 140 BC to 120 BC, as Prof. Lassen's chronology says that Menandros seiged Ayodhyā in 144 BC. Bhandarkar differs slightly from him taking the very earlier years of Menandros for the examples *aruṇadyavanaḥ sāketam* and *aruṇadyavano mādhyamikām*.

Thus Bhandarkar concludes that Patañjali lived in the reign of Puṣyamitra and that he, probably, wrote his commentary on the 3rd book of the *Aṣṭādhyāyī* between 144 BC and 142 BC. This also agrees with the conclusion of Prof. Goldstücker that the author of the *Mahābhāṣya* flourished after the extinct of Maurya dynasty.

Prof. S.D. Joshi

Prof. S.D. Joshi, in 1976, in the introductary part of his book, viz., *Patañjali's Vyākaraṇa Mahābhāṣya, Anabhihitāhnika* has analysed the views of the earlier eminent researchers and gives his own opinion. He raises his doubt against the examples about their authorship, historical identity and the confirmation about the dates. He enlists some examples as follows:

(a) *śakyavanam* (*Mbh*, 2.4.10)

(b) *mauryehiraṇyārthibhirarcāḥ prakalpitāḥ*, (*Mbh*, 5.3.99)

(c) *śākapārthiva* (A *vārttika*)

(d) *śakandhu* (A *vārttika*)

(e) *puṣyamitrasabhā, candraguptasabhā* (*Mbh*, 1.1.68)

(f) *puṣyamitro yajate yājakā yājayanti* (*Mbh*, -3-1-26)

(g) *aruṇadyavanaḥ sāketam, aruṇadyavano mādhyamikān* (*Mbh*, 3.2.111)

(h) *iha puṣyamitraṁ yājayāmaḥ* (*Mbh*, 3.2.123)

According to him, these examples cannot be crucial to fix the date of Patañjali as some of these may not be Patañjali's own words or may not be historically identifiable or some events referred to are not datable. So, isolation, these examples cannot give any clue to fix the date of Patañjali. But, together, these lines imply that either Kātyāyana or Patañjali must have lived in this period. Prof. Joshi is of the opinion that we should consider Kātyāyana's period from the above examples rather than Patañjali's period. Because, the explanation on the rule P. 2.4.10 *śūdrāṇāmanirvasitānām*[8] gives the hint of much later period for Patañjali. He takes the support of De La Vallée Poussin and says that around 150 BC, the Indians were not sufficiently familiar with the Śakas to include their names together with those of the Greeks in a Sanskrit compound and as the Śakas first invaded India around 120 BC, Patañjali cannot be before first century BC. Under the king, Maues, the first known Śaka king in India, Śakas occupied Taxila at around 85 BC and seem to have reached Mathurā by about 60 BC. In this context, Prof. Joshi refers to "Tarn, *GBJ*, p. 322", which dates the conquest of Taxila not long before 77 BC.

So, thus, Prof. Joshi opines about the upper limit of *Bhāṣya* as 85 BC. And about the examples like *aruṇadyavanaḥ sāketam*, etc., he says the example is not very convincing to fix the date, depending upon the same. Because, the same example is quoted in *Kāśikāvṛtti*. So, this is sufficient to show that the inroads of the Yavanas produced such an impression that the seiges could be used as a stock-example in grammar. The same goes for the examples in which mention is made of Puṣyamitra's *aśvamedha* sacrifice.

The same arguments, Prof. Joshi has put again in 1980, in

---

8. यैर्भुंके पात्रं संस्कारेण शुद्धयति तेऽनिरवसिताः "Those after whose eating the dish becomes pure (again) by cleaning (are called) अनिरवसित, i.e., not banned from the society."

   When there is a *dvandva* compound of this kind of words, singular form is prescribed by the rule शूद्राणामनिरवसितानाम् (2.4.10), for example 'शक्यवनम्'.

   Reference from the footnote no. 120, of the article "The contribution of R.G. Bhandarkar to the study of Sanskrit Grammar". In the book *Sanskrit and Indian Studies, Essays in Honour of Daniel H.H. Ingalls*, p. 58.

the book *Sanskrit and Indian Studies*, which is a collection of essays in honour of Daniel H.H. Ingalls, consisting an article viz., "The Contribution of R.G. Bhandarkar to the Study of Sanskrit Grammar". Further, in another of his book, viz, *Patañjali's Vyākaraṇa Mahābhāṣya: Paspaśāhnika*, on the account of the explanation of the *Vārttika, siddhe śabdārtha-sambandhe*, he has clearly mentioned both the upper limit and the lower limit as 85 BC and AD 250, respectively.

Dr. B.N. Puri (1957)

Before Prof. S.D. Joshi, another eminent scholar, viz., Dr. B.N. Puri has to opine something, in this regard. In his book, viz., *India in the Time of Patañjali*, he has refreshed the views of many scholars who have fixed different dates to Patañjali, such as Böhtlingk — 200 BC, Max Müller — 200 BC, Goldstücker and Bhandarkar — 144-142 BC and Keith — 150 BC. Though directly he has not specified the date of *Mahābhāṣya*, his analysis regarding the period of Puṣyamitra's reign is from 185 BC to 174 BC as he quotes from P.C. Bagchi and supports the same view. Thus, this must be his idea that Patañjali lived within that period and *Mahābhāṣya* is written in the meantime.

Yudhiṣṭhira Mīmāṁsaka

Apart from the modern approach of research, we should have a glance at what the Indian traditional approach concludes, which Ācārya Yudhiṣṭhira Mīmāṁsaka takes the lead. He is far from believing the thought, presented from the West. In his book *Vyākaraṇa Śāstra Kā Itihāsa*, he stretches the time of Patañjali during as early as 2000 BC. It is also interesting to study the way he establishes his own view and refutes the theories presented by the modern approach. His objections are as follows:

(a) There is no direct mention in the *Mahābhāṣya* that

Puṣyamitra is a king or belonging to Śuṅga dynasty. Also, it is not mentioned that Puṣyamitra performed any *aśvamedha* sacrifice. So, this name also might have been used fictionally as Devadatta, Yajñadatta or Vasumitra, etc.

(b) If there is any claim about the example, *iha puṣyamitra yājayāmaḥ*, i.e., *iha* means Pāṭaliputra, then in the very next sentence, *iha adhīmahe*, would mean Patañjali, *et al*, during the period of Puṣyamitra's *aśvamedha* sacrifice, 'we are studying in Pāṭaliputra'. So, the view that Patañjali wrote *Bhāṣya* during that period would go contrary to the facts. How can, while studying, Patañjali write such a huge and authentic Bhāṣya.

(c) Regarding the sentence *candraguptasabhā*, Mīmāṁsaka finds it not available in many manuscripts and, wherever it is found, it is after the sentence *puṣyamitrasabhā*. But the chronology of Candragupta and Puṣyamitra is just the opposite. So this cannot be an authentic clue.

(d) Yudhiṣṭhira Mīmāṁsaka disagrees with the view that the word *vṛṣala* means Candragupta. He means *adharmātmā* (evil-being) which, according to him, is found in so many texts earlier to *Bhāṣya*. So, even the sentences, like *jeyo vṛṣalaḥ* and *kāṇḍībhūtaṁ vṛṣalakulam* in *Bhāṣya* (1.1.50) and (6.3.61), respectively, cannot be the proof to identify Candragupta and *vṛṣala*, so that it can be assumed that Patañjali belonged to a later period than Candragupta.

(e) Even the sentence *mauryahiraṇyārthibhirarcāḥ prakalpitāḥ* (P.5.3.99) cannot be solid to prove the subsequent period of Candragupta Maurya, because, according to many commentators of *Bhāṣya*, Maurya means "architect", *śilpī*.

(f) There is no direct mention of any king in the sentence *aruṇadyavanaḥ sāketam* and *aruṇa-dyavano mādhyamikān.* Moreover, there was mention of an early emperor named Kālayavana, who attacked a major part of India and was killed by Śrī Kṛṣṇa. This reference is found in *Manu-Smṛti* (10.43/44). This proves that the Indian Āryans were familiar with the Yavanas from quite early period. So, we cannot say that it is Menandros only who beseiged Ayodhyā and Mādhyamikā, for the first time. According to him, even there are references of Yavanas in the *Rāmāyaṇa* and the *Mahābhārata*.

(g) The refutation of line, fixed by the Western scholars, is further strengthened by the proof of what Bhartṛhari[9] and Kalhaṇa[10] provide. Both have mentioned that Candrācārya has revived the *Mahābhāṣya* which was almost ceased from the tradition. So, when he brought it back to the tradition he might have restructured it and some interpolations are obvious.

Thus, refuting on the above grounds, Ācārya Mīmāṁsaka goes on fixing a very early date of Patañjali, taking the device of ancient Indian researches. Those are as follows.

Nature's Principle in Human being's Average Age

Caraka Saṁhitā, a treatise on *Āyurveda* confines the average age of human being to be hundred years, in the initial age of *kaliyuga*. That average age gets reduced by one year in each

9. पर्वतादागमं लब्ध्वा भाष्यबीजानुसारिभिः।
स नीतो बहुशाखत्वं चन्द्राचार्यादिभिः पुनः॥ (वाक्यपदीय of भर्तृहरि, 2.489)

10. चन्द्राचार्याभिर्लब्ध्वादेशं तस्मात्तदागमम्।
प्रवर्तितं महाभाष्यं स्व च व्याकरणं कृतम्॥ (राजतरङ्गिणी of कल्हण, 1-176).

century. In Paspaśāhnika of *Mahābhāṣya*, Patañjali says, *kiṁ punaradyatve yaḥ sarvathā ciraṁ jīvati varṣaśataṁ jīvati*. This implies that the average age, at that time, was not hundred years. Some years were definitely reduced. To support the view of Caraka, he finds a similar reference in the Bible,[11] that man's average age is seventy years and by some penance that can be extended up to ten years. So the average age from the beginning of *kaliyuga* had been reduced by thirty years at that time of the Bible. That means, according to Caraka's calculations, 3000 years are passed at the time of the Bible. And as Patañjali hints that it is only ten years less than at the beginning of *kali*, i.e., 1000 years are passed. So, *Mahābhāṣya*'s time is 2000 years before the Bible's time.

Hint of Samudragupta in Kṛṣṇacarita

In *Kṛṣṇacarita* of Samudragupta, which is partly available, there is a chronology of sage poets and royal poets, where Samudragupta mentions Patañjali, as earlier to Bhāṣa. "According to the Indian history, the time of Bhāṣa should be 1500 years before Vikram Saṁvat,"[12] thus opines Mīmāṁsaka. So, as Patañjali is supposed to be earlier to Bhāṣa, he definitely has to be before that and, therefore, should belong to near about 2000 BC.

Thus, Ācārya Mīmāṁsaka concludes, with a very early date of Patañjali, and refutes the illustrations, based upon which the modern approaches each in the later period,

---

11. Yudhiṣṭhira Mīmāṁsaka translates the Bible as "हमारी आयु के बरस सत्तर तो होते है, और चाहे बल के कारण अस्सी बरस हों, तो भी उन पर का घमण्ड कष्ट और व्यर्थ बात ठहरता है।" in his book *व्याकरण शास्त्र का इतिहास*, p. 347, सुरेन्द्रकुमार कपूर, रामलाल कपूर ट्रस्ट प्रेस, बहालगढ़ जिला सोनीपत (हरियाणा) सं॰ 2030

12. Vikram Saṁvat is Christian era +56.

    Reference from वामन शिवराम आप्टे, *संस्कृत-हिन्दी कोश*, छात्र संस्करण। p. 1047, under संवत्.

considering the interpolations made by Ācārya Candragomin. This kind of interpolations, according to him, is very familiar in Indian literary tradition, for instance, *Rāmāyaṇa*, *Mahābhārata*, etc.

Conclusion

Before reaching at any fixed point, we should observe the common topic, touched by different scholars, i.e., about Patañjali's authorship of the examples.

Based upon the examples like *aruṇadyavanaḥ sāketam*, *aruṇadyavano mādhyamikān*, *candraguptasabhā*, *puṣyamitrasabhā*, etc., Prof. Goldstücker and Prof. Bhandarkar reach at their conclusion, i.e., about 150 BC. But some scholars like Prof. S.D. Joshi and Ācārya Mīmāṁsaka doubt whether the examples belong to Patañjali or not. Again, these two scholars have still different views. Mīmāṁsaka considers these examples as later interpolations made by Candrācārya while S.D. Joshi considers these as stock examples continuing since long before even from Kātyāyana, which prompts him to fix the time of Patañjali much later and the previously established date of Patañjali, i.e., around 150 BC is actually the date of Kātyāyana.

In this context it will not be wise to take Mīmāṁsaka's view, authoritative, because Keilhorn[13], in his research of the manuscript tradition of *Bhāṣya*, does not find any clue that there is any re-edition of the *Bhāṣya*. And the later scholars have accepted the theory of Keilhorn as authentic. Most

---

13. F. Kielhon (1878) in the article "On the Mahābhāṣya" says, "We may, perhaps, allow a break so far as regards its traditional interpretation, but for the present we are bound to regard the text of the *Mahābhāṣya* as given by our MSS to be the same as it existed about two thousand years ago" in the book *Kleine Schriften*, Franz Steiner Verlay Gmbh. Wiesbaden (1969), p. 169.

recently, George Cardona (1978)[14] has considered the conclusion, reached by Keilhorn, established even refuting the views made by S.D. Joshi that the *Mahābhāṣya* gives the impression of being a hybrid kind of work, a compilation.

Mīmāṁsaka's other views also do not seem to be conclusive. Nature's principle regarding the human age, nowadays seems to be opposite. As the medical science develops, the record of events shows man's average age of living is actually increasing. So the thought, presented by him, seems to be mythical. Again, his reference of Samudragupta's *Kṛṣṇacarita* needs more proof to be considered as a historical document.

So, though there remains a little controversy even among the modern thinkers and researchers, we cannot completely take the orthodox and traditional view as authentic. Despite the controversies among the scholars, hence, the period of Patañjali is to be taken not before second century BC and not after second century AD, in general, and, particularly, at around 150 BC. This view is an established theory which most of the scholars seem to have accepted. Most recently, Johannes Bronkhorst[15] (1987) has assumed the same conclusion, derived from the examples of *aruṇadyavanaḥ sāketam* and *aruṇadyavano mādhyamikām*. But he accepts its validity, till it is proved that these are the examples, introduced by Patañjali only. Otherwise, if these are borrowed from an earlier grammarian, then the suppored date of Patañjali will be at a later date.

Prof. Joshi, in this regard, refers to a very pertinent remark of F. Kielhorn on grammatical examples that, dating a

14. "Still again on the History of Mahābhāṣya" an article by George Cardona published in the Annal of Bhandarkar Oriental Research Institute, Pune, Diamond Jubilee Volume (1978), pp. 79-99.

15. "Three Problems Pertaining to the Mahābhāṣya," a lecture series by Johannes Bronkhorst at Bhandarkar Oriental Research Institute, Poona (1987), pp. 43-44.

grammarian on the strength of his examples, cannot always lead to a safe conclusive result.[16] This seems to be virtually comprehensible. Here, it should be noticed that the examples may not help fixing the lower limit of the date, but, at least, the upper limit can be fixed. So, this, at least, seems to proof the point that Patañjali must have existed before the attack of Yavana on Sāketa and Mādhyamika but, Prof. Joshi rightly remarks that the contemporaneity of the incidents might belong to Kātyāyana and the incidents have become stock examples, continued up to Patañjali and even up to Jayāditya Vāmana. And more mention of the same example in *Kāśikāvṛtti* cannot give the conclusion that the seige of Yavana also occurred at the time of Jayāditya Vāmana.

As Kātyāyana's *Vārttikas* are not designed in the way that along with the rules, examples must be quoted that we cannot be sure that Kātyāyana is earlier to these incidents and first Patañjali has faced them.

Thus, Joshi's view in dating *Mahābhāṣya* seems to be convincing as he has further been able to fix the upper limit of Patañjali, i.e., 85 BC on the strength of the explanation of the word *anirvasita*, i.e., the Śakas and, according to Tarn[17], some Śakas, under the king Maues, who first invaded India in 85 BC. So Patañjali must have been living after that period and there is no harm considering the quoted examples, belonging to Kātyāyana.

---

16. Joshi sums up Kielhorn's view that "dating a grammarian on the strength of his examples cannot always lead to a safe result, because we do not know whether he himself has phrased the example or just took them from the tradition." p. xiv, Introduction of *Patañjali's Mahābhāṣya: Anabhihitāhnika* by Prof. S.D. Joshi, University of Pune, Pune.

17. Reference is from the footnote no.185, p. xxv, Introduction of *Patañjali's Mahābhāṣya: Anabhihitāhnika* by Prof. S.D. Joshi & J.A.F. Roodbergen University of Poona, Poona (1976).

References

Bhandarkar, R.G. (1872), "On the Date of Patañjali and the King in whose reign he lived," in the book *A Reader on the Sanskrit Grammarians* Ed. by J.F. Staal, The MIT Press, Cambridge, Massachusetts and London, England, 1972, pp. 78-81.

Bronkhorst, J. (1987), "Three Problems Pertaining to the Mahābhāṣya", A Lecture Series at Bhandarkar Oriental Research Institute, Poona, pp. 43-44.

Cardona, G. (1978), "Still again on the History of the Mahābhāṣya" in the Annal of Bhandarkar Oriental Research Institute, Diamond Jubilee Volume, Ed. by R.N. Dandekar, pp. 79-99.

———, (1999), *Recent Researches in Pāṇinian Studies*, Motilal Banarasidass, New Delhi, 1999.

Goldstücker, T. (1861), *Pāṇini: His place in Sanskrit Literature, An Investigation*, Ed. by Prof. Surendra Nath Shastri, The Chowkhamba Sanskrit Series Office, Vārāṇasī (1965), pp. 247-58.

Joshi, S.D. (1976), *Patañjali's Vyākaraṇa Mahābhāṣya: Anabhihitāhnika* with co-authorship of J.A.F. Roodbergen, University of Pune, Pune, pp. i-xxiv, Introduction (1979); "The Contribution of R.G. Bhandarkar to the Study of Sanskrit Grammar" in the book *Sanskrit and Indian Studies, Essays in Honour of Daniel H.H. Ingalls*, Ed. M. Nagatomi, B.K. Matilal, J.M. Masson and E. Dimock, D. Reidel Publishing Company, Dordrecht: Holland, Boston: U.S.A., London: England.

Joshi, S.D. (1986), *Patañjali's Vyākaraṇa Mahābhāṣya: Paspaśāhnika*, with co-authorship of J.A.F. Roodbergen, University of Pune, Pune, p. 115.

Kielhorn, F. (1878), "On the Mahābhāṣya" in the book *Kleine Schriften*, Franz Steiner Verlag Gmbh, Wiesbaden (1969), pp. 169-79.

Laddu, S.D. (1981), "A Reconsideration of the History of the Mahābhāṣya" in CASS Studies, Number 6, Ed. S.D. Joshi, University of Poona, Poona (1982), pp. 187-97.

Mīmāṁsaka, Y., *संस्कृत व्याकरण शास्त्र का इतिहास*, Ramlal Kapoor Trust, Bahalgarh, Sonepat, Haryana, pp. 330-49.

Puri, B.N. (1957), *India in the time of Patañjali*, Bharatiya Vidya Bhavan, Bombay, pp. 4-11.

Bibliography

Primary Sources

VEDIC SAṀHITĀS

Atharvaveda Saṁhitā, Ed. Vishva Bandhu, Hoshiarpur, 1960-64.

Ṛgveda Saṁhitā, Ed. N.S. Sontakke and C.G. Kashikar, Poona, 1933-51.

Sāmaveda Saṁhitā, Ed. S.D. Satavalekara, Pardi, 1956.

Taittirīya Saṁhitā, Ed. S.D. Satavalekara, Pardi, 1957.

Vājasaneyī Saṁhitā, Ed. Vasudeva Laxman Sastri Pansikar, Bombay, 1929.

Yajurveda Saṁhitā, Ed. Ravi Prakash Arya, Parimal Publications, Delhi, 2nd Edn., 1999.

BRĀHMAṆAS

Aitareya Brāhmaṇa with Sāyaṇa Bhāṣya published in An.S.S., Poona, 1930-31.

Śatapatha Brāhmaṇa, Ed. Vidyadhara Sarma, Achyuta Grantha Mala, Vārāṇasī, 1937.

Ṣaḍviṁśa Brāhmaṇa, with Sāyaṇa Bhāṣya, Ed. B.R. Sharma, Tirupati, 1967.

Taittirīya Brāhmaṇa with Sāyaṇa Bhāṣya, Published in An.S.S., Poona, 1934-38.

ĀRAṆYAKAS

Aitareya Āraṇyaka, Ed. A.B. Keith, Oxford, 1909.

Taittirīya Āraṇyaka with Sāyaṇa Bhāṣya, Published in An.S.S., Poona, 1926-27.

UPANIṢADS

Aitareya Upaniṣad, *Bṛhadāraṇyakopaniṣad*, *Chāndogyopaniṣad*, *Kaivalyopaniṣad*,

Kaṭhopaniṣad, Kauśitakī Upaniṣad, Kenopaniṣad, Mahānārāyaṇopaniṣad, Māṇḍūkyopaniṣad, Śvetāśvetaropaniṣad, Taittirīya Upaniṣad — One Hundered and twelve Upaniṣads and their Philosophy, Dr. A.N. Bhattacharya, Parimal Publications, Delhi, 2nd Edn., 1999.

VYĀKARAṆA

Amarakoṣa, Ed. Haragovinda Sastri, Chowkhamba Sanskrit Series, Chowkhamba, Vārāṇasī, 1957.

Aṣṭādhyāyī, Ed. Otto Böhtlingk, MLBD, Delhi, Reprint, 2001.

Atharvaprātiśākhya, Ed. Surya Kant, Delhi, 1968.

Daśapādyuṇādivṛtti, Ed. Government Sanskrit College, Banaras, 1943.

Kāśikā, Ed. Jitendra Buddhi, The Varendra Research Society, Rajshahi, 1919-25.

Mahābhāṣya of Patañjali, Nirnayasagar Press, Mumbai, 1932.

Mahābhāṣya of Patañjali, Paspaśāhnika, Introduction, text, translation and notes, University of Pune, Pune, 1986.

Mahābhāṣya of Patañjali, The Samarthāhnika, Ed. S.D. Joshi and J.A.F. Roodbergen, CASS, University of Pune, Pune, 1968.

Mahābhāṣya of Patañjali, The Sthānivadbhāvāhnika, Part I, Ed. S.D. Joshi and J.A.F. Roodbergen, BORI, Pune, 1990.

Mahābhāṣya of Patañjali, Anabhihitāhnika, Ed. S.D. Joshi and J.A.F. Roodbergen, University of Pune, Pune, 1976.

Nirukta, Ed. K.V. Rajwade, Poona, 1940.

Pāṇinīya Śikṣā, text and translation, M. Ghosh, V.K. Publishing Home, New Delhi, 1991.

Siddhānta-Kaumudī, Bhaṭṭojī Dīkṣita, Chowkhamba, Vārāṇasī.

Śrīmadbhāgvatpatañjalikṛta Vyākaraṇamahābhāṣya, Marāṭhī translation by M.M. Vasudevashastri Abhyankar, Deccan Education Society, Pune, 1954.

Taittirīya Prātiśākhya, Ed. W.D. Whitney, Chowkhamba, Vārāṇasī.

The Vyākaraṇa Mahābhāṣya of Patañjali, 3 Vols, Ed. L.F. Keilhorn, Government Central Press, Bombay, 1880-85.

Vākyapadīya of Bharttṛhari, Kāṇḍa II, Ed. K.A. Subrahmania Iyer, MLBD, Delhi, 1983.

Vyākaraṇamahābhāṣya, Ed. Vedavrat, Gurukul, Jhajjiar, Vol. I, 1962.

OTHER WORKS

Parāśaropapurāṇa, Ed. Kapildev Tripathy, Sampurnananda Sanskrit Vishvavidyalaya, Vārāṇasī, 1990.

Raghuvaṁśam, Ed. H.D. Valenkar, Bombay, 1948.

SECONDARY SOURCES

Abhyankar, K.V., *A Dictionary of Sanskrit Grammar*, Baroda Oriental Institute, 1964.

Agrawal, V.S., *Pāṇinikālīna Bhāratavarṣa*, MLBD, Delhi, Vikrama Saṁvat 2012.

———, *India as Known to Pāṇini*, Benaras, 1955.

Banerji, S.C., *Historical Survey of Ancient Indian Grammars* (Sanskrit, Pāli and Prākṛt), Delhi, 1996.

Belvalkar, S.K., *Systems of Sanskrit Grammar*, Bombay, 1915.

Cardona, G., *Pāṇini: A Survey of Research*, MLBD, Delhi, Reprint, 1980.

———, *Recent Researches in Pāṇinian Studies*, MLBD, Delhi, 1998.

———, *Studies in Indian Grammarians*, Chicago, 1969.

Chatterji, K.C., *Technical terms and technique of Sanskrit Grammar*, Poona, 1948, Pt. I.

Das, K.C., *Pāṇinian Approach to Philosophy of Language*, Sanskrit Pustak Bhandar, Calcutta, 1990.

Das, K.S., *Paribhāṣās in the Pāṇinian System of Grammar*, Sanskrit Book Depot, Calcutta, 1986.

Despande, M., *Critical Studies in Indian Grammarian*, Michigan, 1975.

Devasthali, G.V., *Pāṇini and Ṛgvedic Exegesis*, CASS, University of Pune, Pune, 1968.

———, *Anubandhas of Pāṇini*, 1967.

Dvivedi, H.P., *Studies in Pāṇini*, 1978.

Eggeling, J., Ed., *Vardhamāna's Gaṇaratnamahodadhi with the author's commentary*, Reprint, MLBD, Delhi, 1963.

Gaud, V.L., *Pāṇini kī Sthānyādeśa Vyavasthā*, Lokaloka Prakashan, Ghaziabad, 1985.

Gode, P.K., *Studies in Indian Literary History*, 3 Vols., Bhāratīya Vidyā Bhavan, Bombay, 1953-56.

Goldstücker, T., *Pāṇini, his place in Sanskrit literature*, The Pāṇini Office, Allahabad, 1914, Reprint.

Gonda, J., *Aspects of Early Viṣṇuism*, MLBD, Delhi, Reprint, 1969.

Goonatilleke, W., *Pāṇini's eight books of grammatical sūtras*, Education Society Press, Bombay, 1882.

Hemachandra, *Siddha-Haima-Śabdānuśāsana*, Ed. Ganindra Chandra Sagar, Bombay, 1945, Pat I.

Iyer, K.A.S., Ed., *Vākyapadīya of Bharttṛhari*, MLBD, Delhi, 1983.

Joshi, V.L., *Prauḍha Manoramā* with Commentary Śabdaratna; appendices 1-3, Deccan College, Poona, 1964.

Joshi, V.N.S. and Panśikar, W.L., Ed., *The Bhaṭṭīkāvya of Bhaṭṭī with the Commentary of Jayamaṅgalā*, Nirnaya Sagar Press, Bombay, 1928.

Joshi, S.D., *Pāṇini as Variant*, CASS, University of Poona, Pune, 1980.

Kalhaṇa, *Rājtaraṅgiṇī*, Ed. M.A. Stein, Delhi, 1960.

Kane, P.V., *History of Dharmaśāstra*, BORI, Poona, 1930, Vol. 1; 1941, Vol. 2; 1962, Vol. 5, pt. 2.

Kedaranatha, *Pāṇiniyan Vyākaraṇam*, Tadupari Akṣepāśca, Sanskṛt Kāryālaya, Ayodhyā, 1952.

Keith, A.B., *A History of Sanskrit Literature*, Oxford University Press, London, 1920, Reprint 1948.

Kielhorn, L.F., Ed., *The Paribhāṣenduśekhara of Nāgojībhaṭṭa*, The Indu Prakash Press, Bombay, 1868, Revised edition, 1962.

———, tr., *The Paribhāṣenduśekhara of Nāgojībhaṭṭa*, Government Central Book Depot, Bombay, 1874, New edition, 1960.

———, *Kātyāyana and Patañjali: their relation to each-other and to Pāṇini*, The Educational Society, Bombay, 1876, Reprint (Indological Book House, Vārāṇasī), 1963.

Kṣemendra, *Bṛhat Kathāmañjarī*, Calcutta, 1960.

Kunhan Raja, C., *Descriptive Catalogue of Sanskrit manuscripts in the Adyar Library; Vol. VI: Grammar, Prosody and Pexicography* (= ALS60), The Adyar Library, Madras, 1947.

Laddu, S.D., *EVolution of the Sanskrit language from Pāṇini to Patañjali* with reference to the primary formations, CASS, University of Pune, Pune, 1967.

Liebich, B., *Chandravyākaraṇa*, Leipzig, 1902.

Limaye, V.P., *Critical Studies on the Mahābhāṣya*, Vishveshvarananda Vedic Research Institute, Hoshiarpur, Panjab, 1974.

Macdonell, A.A., *A History of Sanskrit Literature*, William Heinemann, London, 1909.

Maxmüller, F., Ed., *The Sacred Books of the East*, The Vedānta Sūtras with Commentary by Śaṅkarācārya, tr. George Thibaut, Part II, Reprint, MLBD, Delhi, 1962.

Mīmāṁsaka, Pt. Y., *Saṁskṛta Vyākaraṇa Śāstra kā Itihāsa*, 3 Vols, Ramlal Kapoor Trust, Sonepat, Haryana, 1973.

Mirashi, V.V., *Laghu-Siddhāntakaumudī*, Part I, MLBD, Delhi, 1967.

Mishra, M., *Critical Study of the Vārttikas of Kātyāyana*, Ph.D. dissertation submitted to the University of Pune, 1992.

Mishra, V., *Vyākaraṇavārttika: eka samīkṣātmaka adhyayana*, Pṛthivī Prakashan, Vārāṇasī, 1970.

Mishra, Pt. V., *Odiā bhāṣāra Purā Tattva*, 1st Edn., 1965.

Narang, S.P., *Bhaṭṭī-Kāvya: A Study*, MLBD, Delhi, 1969.

Nārāyaṇabhaṭṭa., *Prakriyāsarvasva*, Madras, 1941.

Nath, N.C., *Pāṇinian Interpretation of the Sanskrit Language*, BHU, Vārāṇasī, 1969.

Nene G.S., Ed., *Laghuśabdenduśekhara*, Chowkhamba, Benares, 2nd Edn. 1954.

———, *The Śabda Kaustubha*, Vol. II, Chowkhamba, Benares, 1929.

———, *The Prauḍhamanoramā*, Chowkhamba, Benares, 1939.

———, M.M. *Śrīmad-bhaṭṭojī-dīkṣita-Viracitā Vaiyākaraṇa-Siddhānta-Kaumudī Śrī-Vāsudeva-dīkṣita-kṛta-bālamanoramā-Vyākhyā Sahitā*, Chowkhamba, Vārāṇasī, 1958-61.

Nikam, N.A. and Mckeon, R., *Ten Principal Upaniṣads*, Bombay, 1974.

Oldenberg, H., *The Religion of the Veda*, Berlin, 1890.

Palsule, G.B., Ed., *Kavikalpadruma of Vopadeva*, Deccan College, Poona, 1954.

Pansīkar, W.L.S., Ed., *Siddhānta Kaumudī*, Nirnaya Sagar Press, Bombay, 1913.

Paranjape, V.G., *Le Vārttika de Kātyāyana*, Heidelberg, 1922.

Patankar, R.N., *Mahārāṣṭrīya Aṣṭādhyāyī*, Ārya Sanskrit Mudraṇālaya, Pune, 1862.

Pathak, S., *Mahābhāṣyadipikā*, Delhi, 1997.

Phāṭaka, M., *Pāṇinīyaśikṣāyāḥ Śikṣāntaraiḥ Saha Samikṣātmakam adhyayanam*, Chowkhamba, Vārāṇasī, 1969.

Puri, B.N., *India in the line of Patañjali*, Bharatiya Vidya Bhavan, Bombay, 1957.

Ram Gopal, *India of Vedic Kalpasūtras*, MLBD, Delhi, 1983.

Ramsharma, *Vyākaraṇasiddhāntacandrikā*, Benaras, 1939.

Ray, B.L., Ed., *Facets of Vedic Studies*, Kaveri Book Service, New Delhi, 2000.

Renou, L., *Etudes de Pāṇini*, Paris, 1947 and 1951.

———, *Vedic India*, Indological Book House, Delhi, 1971.

Saini, R.S., *Post-Pāṇinian Systems of Sanskrit Grammar*, Parimal Publications, Delhi, 1999.

Sarma, M.K., *Pāṇini, Kātyāyana and Patañjali*, Chowkhamba, Vārāṇasī, 1968.

Sarma, R., *The Aṣṭādhyāyī of Pāṇini*, 1987.

Sastri, S., *Vaidika Vyākaraṇa*, MLBD, Delhi, 1971.

Sathe, M.D., *Pāṇini va Pāṇinīya Vyākaraṇa Sampradāya*, Joshi-Lokhande, Pune, 1984.

Scharfe, H., *Grammatical Literature*, J. Gonda, Ed., *A History of Indian Literature*, Wiesbaden, 1977.

Shukla, S., *Pāṇiniyavyākaraṇa evam Agnipurāṇa men Nirūpita Vyākaraṇa*, J.P. Publishing House, Delhi, 1990.

Subrahmanyam, P.S. and Bhayani, H.C., *Lingustic Society of India*, Deccan College, Pune, 1992.

Swaminathan, V., Ed., *Mahābhāṣya Tīkā*, BHU, Vārāṇasī, 1965.

Thieme, P., *Pāṇini and the Veda*, Printers and Publishers, Allahabad, 1935.

Tripathi, S.N., *Jainendra-Vyākaraṇa*, Kāśī, 1956.

———, *Śākaṭāyana-Vyākaraṇa*, Vārāṇasī, 1971.

Upadhyaya, B., *Saṁskṛta Śāstron kā Itihāsa*, Vārāṇasī, 1969.

Varma, S., *Saṁskṛta Vyākaraṇa kā Udbhava aur Vikāsa*, MLBD, Delhi, 1971.

Vopadeva, *Kavikalpadruma*, Poona, 1954.

Weber, A., *The History of Indian Literature*, Chowkhamba, Vārāṇasī, 1967.

Weber, M., *The Religion of India*, Illinois, 1958.

Whitney, A.B., *The Atharvaveda Prātīśākhya*, Chowkhamba, 1962.

Winternitz, M., *A History of Indian Literature*, Vol. III, Pt. II, Calcutta University, 1963.

Yakṣavarmā, *Abhidhānacintāmaṇī*, Benaras, 1921.

Zimmer, H., *Philosophies of India*, Routledge and Kegan Paul, London, 1951.

ARTICLES

Abhyankar, K.V., "Authorship of the Laghuśabdaratna," The Annals of the Bhandarkar Oriental Research Institute, Poona, 1964, Vol. 45, 152-58.

Belvalkar, S.K., "An Account of the Different Existing Systems of Sanskrit Grammar," Being Vishvanath Narayan Mandlik Gold Medal Prize-Essay for 1909, Poona, 1915.

Bhandarkar, R.G., "On the Date of Patañjali and the King in whose reign he lived," in the book *A Reader on the Sanskrit Grammarians*, Ed. J.F. Staal, The MIT Press, Cambridge, Massachusetts, 1972, 78-81.

Bronkhorst, J., "Three Problems Pertaining to the Mahābhāṣya," A Lecture Series at BORI, Poona, 1987, 43-44.

Cardona, G., "Pāṇini's syntactlic Categories," *Journal of Oriental Institute*, Baroda, 1967, Vol. 16, 201-15.

———, "Still again on the History of the Mahābhāṣya," in the *Annals of Bhandarkar Oriental Research Institute*, Diamond Jubilee Volume, Ed. R.N. Dandekar, 1978, 79-99.

Coward, H. and Raja, K.K. "The Philosophy of the Grammarians," Potter, Karl, Ed., *Encyclopedia of Indian Philosophies*, Vol. V, New Delhi, 1990.

Dange, S.A., "Some Peculiarities of the eastern dialect according to Pāṇini," *Vidarbha Saṁśodhana Maṇḍala Vārṣika*, Nagpur, 1970, 174-98.

Dasgupta, N.N., "Pāṇini and the Yavanas," *Indian Culture*, Vol. 2, 1935, 356-58.

Devasthali, G.V., "Pāṇini and Ṛgvedic exegesis," *The Annals of the Bhandarkar Oriental Research Institute*, Poona, 1968, Vols. 48-49, 7.

Edgren, A.H., "On the Verbal roots of the Sanskrit language and of the Sanskrit Grammarians," *Journal of the American Oriental Society*, Vol. 11, 1885, 1-55.

Fowler, M., "How Ordered are Pāṇini's rules," *Journal of the American Oriental Society*, Vol. 85, 1965, 44-47.

Gonda, J., "Pāṇini and modern lingustics," in *Konks-Numerkund-mäll*, 1973, 337-52.

Hazra, R.C., "Some Observations on the repetition (anuvṛtti) of Śeṣa from Pāṇini's rule ṣaṣṭhī śeṣa," *Journal of the Asiatic Society* (*of Calcutta*), *Letters*, Vol. 22, 1956, 99-131.

Iyer, V.S., "On Variants in the Aṣṭādhyāyī," in the *Proceedings of the International Seminar on Pāṇini*, Ed. S.D. Joshi and S.D. Laddu, University of Poona, Pune, 1982.

Iyer, V.S., "Pāṇini's Use of Semantics," in the *Proceedings of the International Seminar on Pāṇini*, Ed. S.D. Joshi and S.D. Laddu, University of Poona, Pune, 1982.

Jayaswal, K.P., "Dates of Pāṇini and Kātyāyana," *Indian Antiquary*, Vol. 47, 1918, 138.

Joshi, S.D., "Two methods of interpreting Pāṇini," Publications of CASS, A-5, University of Poona, Pune, 1965.

Kanjilal, D.K., "The Picture of ancient India as revealed in Patañjali's Mahābhāṣya," *Indian Historical Quarterly*, Vol. 31, 1955, 375-82.

Keith, A.B., "Pāṇini and the Veda," *Indian Culture*, Vol. 2, 1936, 735-48.

Laddu, S.D., "A reconsideration of the History of the Mahābhāṣya," in CASS, No.6, Ed. S.D. Joshi, University of Poona, Poona, 1982, 187-197.

Max Müller, F., "The Kāśikā," *Indian Antiquary*, 9, 1880, 305-08.

Mookherji, R.K., "History of Sanskrit Literature from the Works of Pāṇini, Kātyāyana and Patañjali," *Indian Antiquary*, 52, 1923, 21-24.

Nawathe, P.D., "Some un-Pāṇinian forms in the Śrauta-Sūtras," *Proceedings of All India Oriental Congress* (1961), 21, Srinagar, 1966, 210-12.

Palsule, G.B., "Pāṇini's treatment of tense and mood formations," CASS Studies, 1, 1972, 173-83.

Raghavan, V., "Chronological notes: Kaiyaṭa and Dhanañjaya," *Journal of Oriental Research*, 19, 1950, 223-24.

Rath, G., "Sentence Individuality, Indian & Western approach," *VIJ*, Hoshiarpur, Punjab University, 1995-96, Vols. XXXIII-XXXIV, 113-26.

Rocher, R., "The Hindu grammarians and linguistic change," *Journal of Oriental Institute*, Baroda, 11, 1962, 260-68.

Swaminathan, V., "The Nirukta and Patañjali," *Proceedings of All-India Oriental Congress* (1961), Srinagar, 21, 1966, 185-209.

Thieme, P., "Pāṇini and Pāṇinīyas," *Journal of American Oriental Society*, 76, 1956, 1-23.

Upādhyāya, K., "New Verses of Pāṇini," *Indian Historical Quarterly*, 13, 1937, 167-71.

Varma, S., "Scientific and technical Presentation of Patañjali as reflected in the Mahābhāṣya," *VIJ*, 1, 1963, 1-36.

Whitney, N.D., "The Atharva-Veda Prātiśākhya, or Śaunakīya Caturādhyāyekā: text, translation and notes", *JAOS* 7, 1862, 333-615; Reprint, Chowkhamba, Vārāṇasī, 1962.

JOURNALS, PERIODICALS AND PROCEEDINGS

Adyar Library Bulletin, Madras.

Annals of the Bhandarkar Oriental Research Institute, Poona.

Bhāratīya Vidyā, Bombay.

Bulletin of the Deccan Colleage Research Institute, Poona.

Centre of Advanced Study in Sanskrit Studies, Poona.

Indian Antiquary, Bombay.

Indian Culture, Calcutta.

Indian Historical Quarterly, Calcutta.

Jagannātha Jyothi, SJSU, Puri.

Journal of the American Oriental Society, New Haven.

Journal of Oriental Research, Madras.

Journal of the Oriental Institute, Baroda.

Proceedings of the All-India Oriental Conference, Poona.

Viśveśvarānand Indological Journal, Hoshiarpur, Punjab.

Viśva-Saṁskṛtam, Hoshiarpur, Punjab.

FELICITATION AND COMMEMORATION VOLUMES

B.C. Law Felicitation Volume, 2 Vols., 1945-46, (1. Calcutta: The Indian Research Institute, 2. Poona: BORI).

Gaṅganātha Jhā Commemoration Volume, Oriental Book Agency, Poona, 1937.

K.M. Munshi Diamond Jubilee Volume, Pb. 1, 1948.

P.V. Kane Felicitation Volume, Oriental Book Agency, Poona, 1941.

R.N. Dandekar Felicitation Volume, Popular Prakashan, Bombay, 1969.

S.K. Belvalkar Felicitation Volume, MLBD, Vārāṇasī, 1957.

S.M. Katre Felicitation Volume, 1968-69.

S. Varma Felicitation Volume, VVRI, Hoshiarpur, Punjab, 1950.

V. Raghavan Felicitation Volume, Madras, 1967-68.

V.S. Sukthankar Memorial Volume, 1943-44.

W.N. Brown Felicitation Volume, AOS, New Haven, 1962.

Contributors

Saroja Bhate, Department of Sanskrit and Prakrit Languages, University of Pune, Pune-7 (Maharashtra).

P. Narayanan Namboodiri, Department of Sanskrit, University of Calicut, Calicut (Kerala).

Yoshiyuki Iwasaki, Tokyo (Japan).

Shankar Nene, 104, Ketki, Raanwara, Paskan Rd., Bavdhan, Pune-411021 (Maharashtra).

Malhar Kulkarni, Department of Sanskrit and Prakrit Languages, University of Pune, Pune-7 (Maharashtra).

Jatindramohan Mishra, Department of Sanskrit and Prakrit Languages, University of Pune, Pune-7 (Maharashtra).

Bidyut Lata Ray, *Divyadyuti*, Debottar Colony, Nayagarh, 752069 (Orissa).

Krutibas Rath, Librarian, Nayagarh College, Nayagarh, 752069 (Orissa).

Index